Culture and Governance in the Local Church

Stewarding Conviction Under Biblical Authority

Examining Church Culture through the Lens of the LCSM10 Governance Model

Dr. Nathanael J. Lucas

Published by Nathanael J. Lucas
Printed in the United States of America

ISBN 979-8-9945041-6-1

Author's Note:

This work reflects more than a decade of leadership practice, research, and applied governance experience. While tools and technologies assist in drafting and organization, the framework, arguments, and conclusions are the product of sustained reflection and lived practice.

For more information about my consulting work and resources for small organizations, please visit:

www.managementactiongroup.com

The Cascade of the LCSM10

The Foundational Structure for This Work

The LCSM10 leadership model is built upon a cascading framework of organizational alignment. Each layer builds upon the one before it, shaping the environment in which leadership decisions and organizational behavior occur. The following structure forms the foundation for the discussion of culture in this work.

Values
Define the governing convictions of leadership.

Vision
Defines the direction those convictions pursue.

Mission
Defines the work performed to pursue that direction.

Culture
The shared behavioral environment that emerges as people repeatedly live out the mission under shared convictions.

Strategy
The organized approach used to guide that culture toward effective results.

Policy
The structural guardrail that protects alignment and prevents cultural drift.

Culture forms naturally as a congregation repeatedly lives out its mission under shared convictions. Leadership does not manufacture culture directly. Instead, leadership recognizes the culture that emerges, guides it through strategy, and protects it through policy.

This framework provides the structural foundation for the chapters that follow.

PART I
Foundational Definitions and Theological Grounding

Culture in the local church cannot be addressed superficially. It cannot be reduced to atmosphere, personality, or preference. Before examining visible behaviors, worship environments, speech patterns, or leadership posture, we must establish theological and structural clarity. Culture is not an accessory to church life. It is the visible manifestation of what a congregation truly believes, repeatedly practices, and consistently tolerates.

This section establishes the foundation upon which the rest of this work stands. If culture is misunderstood at the definitional level, every corrective effort that follows will be misdirected. Many churches attempt to "improve culture" without first defining it. Others attempt to strengthen governance without rooting it in biblical authority. The result is confusion, inconsistency, and eventually fragmentation.

Culture in the local church must be defined biblically, not sociologically alone. Scripture does not use the modern term culture, yet it consistently addresses patterns of conduct, communal formation, holiness, order, and governance. The early church was marked by continued doctrine, fellowship, breaking of bread, and prayer, Acts 2:42. These repeated patterns formed identity. Identity formed expectation. Expectation formed culture.

Governance, likewise, must be defined under Scripture. Governance is not corporate importation into church life. It is stewardship under Christ's headship. Colossians 1:18 declares that

Christ is the head of the body, the church. Authority in the local church is therefore delegated, accountable, and answerable. Leaders do not invent standards. They steward them.

Conviction precedes conduct. Luke 6:45 teaches that out of the abundance of the heart the mouth speaketh. What is treasured internally becomes visible externally. In congregational life, this principle is multiplied. The repeated expressions of leadership conviction form the patterned behavior of the church body. When conviction is clear and enforced, culture stabilizes. When conviction weakens or remains unenforced, conduct fragments.

This section will therefore define culture, governance, authority, stewardship, conviction, and formation from a biblical framework. It will establish that culture is not declared but formed, not aspirational but observable, not cosmetic but structural. It will also demonstrate that governance under biblical authority is not control, but protection; not rigidity, but stewardship; not dominance, but accountability before God.

If the local church is to steward conviction faithfully, it must first understand what culture truly is and how Scripture shapes its governance. Only then can visible behaviors be examined with clarity rather than reaction. Only then can correction be applied without legalism.

This foundation is necessary. Without it, the discussion of worship style, speech, leadership posture, reverence, hospitality, or discipline becomes preference-driven rather than principle-driven. With it, those same discussions become theological, structural, and accountable before God.

Culture in the local church is the visible testimony of what leadership truly believes about Scripture, holiness, authority, and stewardship. Governance is the means by which those convictions are protected and embodied. This work begins, therefore, not with behavior, but with belief; not with atmosphere, but with authority; not with critique, but with foundation.

Chapter One
Defining Culture in the Local Church

Culture in the local church must be defined carefully, biblically, and structurally. If culture is reduced to atmosphere, personality, creativity, or generational preference, it becomes unstable and subjective. If it is defined merely as "the way we do things around here," it remains descriptive but not theological. In the local church, culture is neither accidental nor neutral. It is the repeated pattern of conduct that emerges from shared conviction under leadership authority.

Scripture consistently connects belief with behavior. Jesus teaches in Luke 6:45 that out of the abundance of the heart the mouth speaketh. What is treasured internally becomes visible externally. This principle applies not only to individuals but to congregations. A church's speech patterns, worship posture, leadership tone, hospitality practices, and disciplinary responses all reveal what the body collectively believes. Culture is therefore not what a church claims to value, but what it consistently embodies.

Culture is also corporate, not merely personal. The church is described as a body in 1 Corinthians 12:12–27, functioning together under Christ as head. Shared doctrine, shared worship, shared correction, and shared mission create shared patterns. Those patterns form expectation. Expectation forms culture. When Acts 2:42 records that the early believers continued steadfastly in doctrine, fellowship, breaking of bread, and prayer, it is describing more than activity. It is describing formation. Repetition formed identity. Identity shaped conduct.

In the local church, culture is not established by a single sermon series or leadership announcement. It is formed through what is repeatedly taught, modeled, rewarded, tolerated, and corrected. Galatians 6:7 reminds us that whatsoever a man soweth, that shall he also reap. The same principle applies corporately. A congregation reaps the culture it consistently sows through governance and example.

It is also important to distinguish between stated culture and lived culture. Titus 1:16 warns of those who profess that they know God, but in works they deny him. The local church can publish vision, mission, and value statements while simultaneously embodying patterns that contradict them. Culture exposes this gap. It is the visible evidence of alignment or misalignment between confession and conduct.

Therefore, culture in the local church may be defined as the observable pattern of shared conduct that flows from enforced conviction under biblical authority. It is not decorative. It is not cosmetic. It is not marketing language. It is the lived testimony of what the congregation truly believes about holiness, authority, reverence, community, and obedience.

If culture is not defined at this level, it will be shaped unintentionally. If it is defined biblically and governed intentionally, it becomes a stewarded expression of conviction rather than a byproduct of preference. This definition provides the necessary framework for everything that follows.

Culture as Repeated Conduct

Culture in the local church is not created solely by intention. It is formed through repetition. What is said once may inspire. What is the repeated forms expectation? What becomes expected becomes normalized. What is normalized becomes culture.

Jesus states in Luke 6:45 (KJV), "A good man out of the good treasure of his heart bringeth forth that which is good… for of the abundance of the heart his mouth speaketh." The principle is clear. Internal conviction produces external expression. When applied corporately, this truth reveals that a congregation's repeated speech, tone, posture, and priorities expose its collective heart. The heart is unseen, but conduct is visible. Over time, repeated conduct becomes the defining character of the body.

James reinforces this connection in James 2:17 (KJV), "Even so faith, if it hath not works, is dead, being alone." Faith that remains abstract is no longer credible. A belief that never manifests in behavior is not merely incomplete; it is lifeless. In the context of the local church, repeated behavior demonstrates what is truly believed. If holiness is preached but casual irreverence is repeated, the repetition will shape culture more than the sermon. If unity is declared but gossip is tolerated, repeated speech will define the environment.

Culture is therefore not formed by mission statements, but by patterns. It is shaped by the tone of the pulpit week after week, the way leaders consistently respond to conflict, the posture of worship practiced regularly, and the expectations continually enforced. A single moment does not create culture. A pattern does.

This is why governance matters. Repetition does not occur accidentally. It is reinforced or corrected. When leaders repeatedly celebrate certain behaviors, those behaviors multiply. When leaders repeatedly ignore certain behaviors, those behaviors entrench. Over time, the congregation absorbs what is practiced more than what is proclaimed.

Culture as repeated conduct also explains why informal settings matter. The language used in small groups, the posture of men's gatherings, the tone of staff meetings, and the behavior at the altar are not isolated incidents. If repeated, they become normative.

If normative, they become formative. Repetition teaches more powerfully than intention.

The local church must therefore examine not only what it believes doctrinally, but what it practices consistently. Conduct repeated becomes culture established. If that conduct aligns with Scripture, the culture will reflect biblical conviction. If it contradicts Scripture, the culture will quietly reshape the congregation away from its stated beliefs. Culture is not declared. It is rehearsed. Over time, rehearsal becomes identity.

Culture as Pattern, Not Atmosphere

Culture in the local church is often mistaken for atmosphere. Atmosphere is felt. Culture is formed. The church atmosphere can change from week to week depending on the music, attendance, or emotion. Culture is revealed over time through consistent patterns of belief and behavior. When culture is reduced to atmosphere, it becomes subjective and unstable. When it is understood as a pattern, it becomes observable and measurable.

Romans 12:2 (KJV) instructs, "And be not conformed to this world: but be ye transformed by the renewing of your mind…" Conformity and transformation are both patterned processes. Conformity happens gradually through repeated exposure and imitation. Transformation occurs through renewal and disciplined reorientation of thought. In either case, behavior follows belief. The apostle Paul is not addressing mood. He is addressing the formation. The church is called to resist worldly patterns and embody renewed ones. Culture, therefore, is the visible pattern of either conformity or transformation. Be transformed through the infilling of God's Holy Spirit.

Philippians 1:27 (KJV) reinforces this pattern language: "Only let your conversation be as it becometh the gospel of Christ…" The word "conversation" in this context refers to conduct, citizenship, and manner of life. Paul calls the church to live in a way that corresponds to the gospel they confess. This is not an appeal to emotional tone. It is a call to patterned alignment. The church's behavior must match its doctrine. Over time, that alignment forms a recognizable culture.

Atmosphere can be energetic, quiet, warm, or intense. None of these defines culture. A church may feel welcoming yet tolerate partiality. It may feel vibrant yet neglect holiness. It may feel reverent yet avoid correction. The atmosphere is immediate. Pattern is cumulative. Culture is cumulative.

When worship gatherings rely on sensory stimulation, lighting, volume, or aesthetic design, atmosphere may intensify. Yet the question remains: what patterns are being formed? Are congregants being trained to participate or to observe? To evaluate experience or to pursue obedience? To seek emotional uplift or doctrinal depth? Repeated patterns answer those questions over time.

Understanding culture as a pattern also shifts leadership responsibility. Leaders cannot manufacture atmosphere consistently, but they can govern patterns. They can reinforce biblical speech. They can model reverent posture. They can correct divisive behavior. They can prioritize doctrine. Governance operates at the level of pattern, not mood.

Therefore, culture in the local church must be evaluated by repeated conduct that reflects renewed minds and gospel-consistent living. It is not defined by how a room feels in a moment. It is defined by how a congregation lives over time. Where the pattern aligns with Scripture, culture reflects transformation. Where the pattern mirrors the world, culture reveals conformity. Culture is not a feeling. It is a formed way of life.

The Difference Between Stated and Lived Conviction

Every local church possesses stated convictions. These convictions may appear in doctrinal statements, value declarations, membership classes, or pulpit affirmations. Yet the presence of stated belief does not guarantee embodied belief. The difference between stated and lived conviction is the space where culture is either validated or exposed.

Titus 1:16 (KJV) provides a sober warning: "They profess that they know God; but in works they deny him…" Profession and practice can diverge. A confession may be orthodox while conduct remains inconsistent. In the context of the local church, this divergence does not remain private. It becomes corporate. When a congregation declares holiness but tolerates irreverence, the lived pattern contradicts the stated conviction. When unity is proclaimed, but gossip persists uncorrected, the culture denies the declaration.

Matthew 15:8 (KJV) echoes this tension: "This people draweth nigh unto me with their mouth, and honoureth me with their lips; but their heart is far from me." External affirmation without internal alignment results in spiritual fragmentation. Words can appear reverent while patterns reveal distance. Over time, repeated contradiction between lips and life produces cultural instability. Members learn, consciously or unconsciously, that language is aspirational but not governing.

This distinction is critical for governance. Leaders often assume that publishing values secures culture. It does not. Culture is not secured by articulation alone, but by enforcement and embodiment. A value statement that is never reinforced through correction, celebration, and modeling becomes symbolic rather than structural. When values are admired but not required, they slowly lose authority.

Lived conviction is demonstrated through repeated obedience. It appears in how leaders handle conflict, how discipline is applied, how money is allocated, how sacred space is treated, and how speech is regulated. These patterns either confirm or contradict the church's stated beliefs. Over time, congregants respond not to what is written, but to what is practiced.

The difference between stated and lived conviction also shapes credibility. A church that speaks clearly yet acts inconsistently loses moral authority. Conversely, a church whose conduct aligns with its confession strengthens its witness. Integrity is not achieved through the volume of declarations, but through the alignment of patterns.

In the local church, stated conviction informs aspiration. Lived conviction forms culture. Governance exists to close the gap between the two. When belief and behavior align, culture stabilizes under the authority of the Bible. When they diverge, culture fragments and trust erodes. The integrity of the church depends not merely on what it professes, but on what it consistently practices.

Why Culture Forms Whether Led or Not

Culture in the local church is not optional. It does not wait for intentional leadership. It does not pause until values are clarified. Culture forms whether it is governed or neglected. The only question is whether it forms intentionally under biblical authority or unintentionally under default influences.

Galatians 6:7–8 (KJV) establishes a governing principle: "Be not deceived; God is not mocked: for whatsoever a man soweth, that shall he also reap." This principle applies both corporately and individually. What a church repeatedly sows in speech, posture, correction, reverence, worship practice, and leadership tone will inevitably be reaped in congregational identity. If holiness is sown, holiness will grow. If casual irreverence is sown, irreverence will normalize. If discipline is neglected, disorder will multiply. There is no neutral ground.

This is why culture does not require permission to form. It is formed through repetition, whether those repetitions are directed or accidental. When leaders fail to define expectations, informal norms emerge. When correction is avoided, tolerated behaviors solidify. When doctrine is softened, conviction weakens. The absence of intentional governance does not prevent culture from forming; it merely guarantees that it will form without direction.

Judges 2:10 (KJV) provides a sobering historical example: "And there arose another generation after them, which knew not the LORD, nor yet the works which he had done for Israel." The prior generation had witnessed deliverance and covenant instruction. Yet when those truths were not intentionally reinforced and transmitted, a new pattern emerged. Cultural memory weakened. Knowledge diminished. Behavior followed. The result was not immediate collapse, but gradual departure.

The lesson is structural. Culture cannot be inherited passively. It must be reinforced actively. When foundational convictions are not repeatedly taught and embodied, a different culture will take their place. Silence becomes instruction. Inconsistency becomes expectation. Neglect becomes formation.

Leadership, therefore, carries responsibility not only for what is taught, but for what is allowed to become normative. If governance is absent, other forces will govern: generational preferences, broader societal trends, personality, or convenience. Culture does not remain undefined. It settles into the path of least resistance.

In the local church, intentional leadership under Scripture is not an exercise in control. It is an exercise in stewardship. To refuse to shape culture deliberately is to surrender it unintentionally. Galatians reminds us that sowing produces harvest. Judges remind us that failure to reinforce conviction produces forgetting. Both passages testify to the same reality: culture forms whether or not it is led. The wise steward recognizes this inevitability and governs accordingly.

Culture as the Visible Evidence of Belief

Culture in the local church is not hidden. It is observable. It may not be formally documented, but it is publicly displayed. Over time, a congregation's behavior becomes visible evidence of what it truly believes. Where belief and conduct align, culture reflects integrity. Where belief and conduct diverge, culture reveals contradiction.

In Matthew 7:16–20 (KJV), Jesus states, "Ye shall know them by their fruits... Wherefore by their fruits ye shall know them." Fruit is not the intention. It is an outcome. It is not an aspiration. It is a manifestation. The fruit of a tree exposes its nature. In the same way, the fruit of a church exposes its convictions. The patterns of speech, reverence, worship posture, discipline, generosity, hospitality, and leadership tone become visible indicators of theological reality.

James 2:18 (KJV) reinforces this connection: "Yea, a man may say, Thou hast faith, and I have works: shew me thy faith without thy works, and I will shew thee my faith by my works." Faith is not demonstrated by declaration alone. It is demonstrated by embodiment. This principle extends beyond individual spirituality into congregational identity. A church's culture shows its faith. The way it handles correction shows its faith. The way it treats sacred moments shows its faith. The way it stewards resources shows its faith.

This reality places culture within the realm of accountability. A belief that remains invisible cannot be evaluated. Belief that produces fruit can. If a church affirms biblical authority yet consistently prioritizes preference, the fruit exposes the true governing influence. If a church proclaims holiness yet normalizes casual irreverence, the fruit reveals a deeper inconsistency. Culture becomes the measurable expression of internal conviction.

This is why governance cannot ignore behavior. It is not enough to defend doctrinal orthodoxy on paper. Orthodoxy must produce orthopraxy. Doctrine must form discipline. Theology must shape tone. When fruit contradicts confession, correction becomes necessary. When fruit confirms confession, stability strengthens.

Culture, therefore, is not peripheral to belief. It is a belief made visible over time. It is the cumulative fruit of repeated conviction. Leadership must understand this clearly. The congregation will be known, not by what it claims, but by what it consistently produces.

Culture stands as testimony. It either confirms the authority of Scripture within the body or reveals that another authority has taken root.

Chapter Two
Defining Governance Under Biblical Authority

Governance in the local church must be carefully defined, because the term is often misunderstood. In secular settings, governance may refer to corporate management, regulatory systems, or executive control. In the church, governance is not the importation of corporate hierarchy. It is stewardship under Christ's authority. It is the ordered responsibility to guard doctrine, protect the flock, and ensure that conduct aligns with Scripture.

Colossians 1:18 (KJV) declares, "And he is the head of the body, the church." Governance begins here. Christ is not a symbolic head. He is the actual head. Authority in the local church is therefore delegated, not inherent. Leaders do not invent standards. They submit to them. They do not rule independently. They steward under divine accountability. Governance is exercised beneath Scripture, not above it.

Second Timothy 3:16–17 (KJV) further establishes the governing framework: "All scripture is given by inspiration of God, and is profitable for doctrine, for reproof, for correction, for instruction in righteousness." Scripture governs doctrine, correction, and instruction. Governance that does not flow from Scripture becomes preference-driven. Governance that flows from Scripture becomes principled and stable. Biblical authority is not advisory. It is final.

Order in the church is not optional. First Corinthians 14:40 (KJV) instructs, "Let all things be done decently and in order." Order is not the enemy of spiritual vitality. It is the protector of it. Throughout Scripture, God establishes structure to preserve covenant faithfulness. In Exodus 18, Moses appoints leaders to prevent chaos. In Acts 6, deacons are appointed to protect unity. Structure exists to safeguard mission, not to suppress it.

Governance must also be distinguished from control. Mark 10:42–45 records Christ's instruction that leadership in His kingdom does not mirror worldly domination. Authority in the church is not coercive, but accountable. First Peter 5:2–3 (KJV) instructs elders to feed the flock, "not as being lords over God's heritage, but being ensamples to the flock." Governance is exercised through example, instruction, and correction, not intimidation.

Yet governance carries weight. Hebrews 13:17 (KJV) reminds believers to obey those who have the rule over you, "for they watch for your souls, as they that must give account." Accountability before God anchors leadership responsibility. Governance is not casual oversight. It is spiritual stewardship with eternal implications.

Defining governance under biblical authority clarifies its purpose. Governance protects doctrine. It preserves order. It corrects deviation. It reinforces conviction. It ensures that the church's culture reflects Scripture rather than shifting preferences. Without governance, culture drifts toward convenience. With biblical governance, culture is intentionally stewarded.

Governance in the local church is therefore the structured stewardship of conviction under the authority of Christ and His Word. It is not corporate imitation. It is a covenant responsibility. It does not replace God's work. It protects what God has entrusted.

Biblical Authority as the Highest Governing Standard

Governance in the local church must begin with a non-negotiable premise: Scripture is the highest governing authority. Not preference. Not tradition. Not personality. Not cultural momentum.

If biblical authority is not functionally supreme, governance becomes unstable, and culture becomes negotiable.

Second Timothy 3:16–17 (KJV) declares, "All scripture is given by inspiration of God, and is profitable for doctrine, for reproof, for correction, for instruction in righteousness: That the man of God may be perfect, throughly furnished unto all good works." Scripture does not merely inspire devotion. It governs doctrine. It reproves the error. It corrects deviation. It instructs righteousness. In other words, Scripture establishes standards and enforces alignment.

If Scripture is profitable for correction, then governance must include correction. If Scripture is profitable for instruction in righteousness, then governance must aim at righteousness, not comfort. Biblical authority is not a decorative citation at the beginning of a sermon. It is the structural framework for decision-making, policy formation, discipline, worship practice, and leadership conduct.

Colossians 1:18 (KJV) adds the second pillar: "And he is the head of the body, the church." Christ is not the advisory head. He is the governing head. His Word expresses His authority. Therefore, to subordinate Scripture to cultural trends or congregational pressure is not merely an administrative compromise. It is a functional displacement of Christ's headship.

This principle has practical implications. When disputes arise, Scripture must decide. When worship methods are debated, Scripture must shape the evaluation. When discipline becomes uncomfortable, Scripture must remain the standard. When growth pressures increase, Scripture must still govern priorities. Biblical authority cannot be selectively applied without weakening governance.

The local church does not create truth. It receives truth. It does not revise righteousness. It submits to righteousness. Governance under biblical authority requires humility from leadership and clarity for the congregation. Leaders are stewards of revelation, not its authors.

When Scripture is clearly taught, consistently applied, and courageously enforced, culture stabilizes under a fixed authority. When Scripture is selectively applied or softened, culture shifts according to the loudest voice or strongest preference. The difference is not subtle. One produces conviction. The other produces negotiation.

Biblical authority must therefore function as the highest governing standard in doctrine, discipline, worship, leadership conduct, and communal life. Without this foundation, governance becomes managerial. With it, governance becomes theological stewardship under Christ's headship.

Order and Structure in Scripture

Order in the local church is not a modern administrative invention. It is a biblical principle. From the earliest pages of Scripture, God establishes structure to preserve clarity, protect responsibility, and sustain faithfulness. Disorder is not neutral. It produces confusion, fatigue, and fragmentation. Order protects both mission and people.

First Corinthians 14:40 (KJV) states plainly, "Let all things be done decently and in order." This instruction appears within a discussion of worship practices. Spiritual gifts were active. Participation was vibrant. Yet Paul insists that spiritual vitality must be governed. Order does not suppress the work of the Spirit. It safeguards it. Without order, worship devolves into competition and distraction. With order, worship becomes edifying and intelligible.

The principle extends beyond worship gatherings. Order reflects clarity of responsibility and structure of authority. Exodus 18:21–23 records Jethro's counsel to Moses to appoint capable men over thousands, hundreds, fifties, and tens. The purpose was not bureaucracy for its own sake. It was preservation. Moses was overwhelmed. The people were waiting. Without structure, exhaustion threatened leadership, and frustration threatened the community. Structure distributed responsibility and stabilized governance.

This biblical pattern demonstrates that structure is not the opposite of spirituality. It is the container that allows spiritual life to flourish without collapsing under its own weight. When roles are undefined, authority unclear, and processes inconsistent, culture becomes reactive. Conflict escalates. Fatigue increases. Informal power structures emerge. Order prevents these outcomes.

In the local church, order includes defined leadership roles, clear accountability, established processes for discipline, thoughtful worship design, and intentional delegation. These are not corporate impositions. They are biblical expressions of stewardship. Structure clarifies who is responsible for teaching, oversight, and service, and how corrections occur.

Order also communicates reverence. When gatherings are intentionally structured, leadership transitions are smooth, and correction follows a defined process, the congregation perceives stability. Disorder, by contrast, signals uncertainty. Over time, repeated disorder forms a culture of unpredictability. Repeated order forms a culture of trust.

Scripture does not equate structure with rigidity. It equates structure with wisdom. Order protects doctrine. It protects leaders from burnout. It protects members from confusion. It protects mission from drift. Governance that reflects biblical order is not oppressive. It is protective.

In the local church, structure is not a replacement for spiritual dependence. It is the means by which spiritual responsibility is carried faithfully. Order and structure in Scripture reveal that God governs intentionally, and those who steward His church must do the same.

Stewardship as Leadership Responsibility

Leadership in the local church is not ownership. It is stewardship. This distinction is essential to understanding governance under biblical authority. Leaders do not possess the church. They are entrusted with it. They do not determine its ultimate direction independently. They are accountable for how faithfully they guard what has been entrusted to them.

First Corinthians 4:2 (KJV) states, "Moreover it is required in stewards, that a man be found faithful." The standard is not creativity. It is not popularity. It is not numerical growth alone. It is faithfulness. A steward manages what belongs to another. In the context of the church, what has been entrusted includes doctrine, discipline, worship, resources, and the souls of the congregation. Faithfulness requires vigilance. It requires correction. It requires clarity.

Hebrews 13:17 (KJV) reinforces the gravity of this responsibility: "Obey them that have the rule over you, and submit yourselves: for they watch for your souls, as they that must give account." Leadership carries spiritual weight. To watch for souls is not a casual assignment. It implies alertness, discernment, and willingness to intervene when necessary. The phrase "as they that must give account" anchors governance in future judgment. Leaders answer to God for how they exercised authority.

Stewardship demands courage. It requires leaders to enforce conviction even when enforcement is uncomfortable. It requires correction when silence would be easier. It requires guarding doctrine when compromise would reduce tension. Faithful stewardship cannot be passive. It must be active and deliberate.

This responsibility extends beyond preaching. It includes shaping culture intentionally. If irrelevance becomes normalized, stewardship requires response. If gossip becomes tolerated, stewardship requires correction. If sacred space becomes casualized, stewardship requires clarity. Culture left unmanaged becomes culture misaligned. Stewardship requires leadership to notice patterns and address them.

Stewardship also includes protection from burnout and disorder. As seen in Exodus 18, structure distributes responsibility so that faithfulness can be sustained. Leaders who attempt to control everything personally eventually weaken governance. Faithful stewardship includes delegation, accountability structures, and clarity of role.

In the local church, leadership is not a platform for influence. It is a trust from God. Governance exercised as stewardship recognizes that every decision, every correction, every allocation of resources, and every tolerance of behavior will one day be reviewed by the One who is Head of the church.

Stewardship is not merely administrative. It is spiritual accountability under divine authority. Leadership responsibility in the local church must therefore be exercised with sobriety, humility, and unwavering commitment to faithfulness.

Governance Versus Control

Governance in the local church must be clearly distinguished from control. Control seeks dominance. Governance seeks faithfulness. Control protects personal authority. Governance protects biblical conviction. When these two are confused, leadership either becomes authoritarian or retreats into passivity out of fear of appearing harsh. Neither reflects the model established in Scripture.

In Mark 10:42–45 (KJV), Jesus contrasts worldly authority with kingdom leadership: "Ye know that they which are accounted to rule over the Gentiles exercise lordship over them… but so shall it not be among you." Authority in Christ's church is not modeled after domination. The Son of Man came not to be ministered unto, but to minister. Leadership is not abolished. It is redefined. Authority remains, but its posture changes. It is exercised through service, not self-exaltation.

First Peter 5:2–3 (KJV) reinforces this distinction: "Feed the flock of God which is among you… neither as being lords over God's heritage, but being ensamples to the flock." Governance requires oversight, but oversight must be shepherding in nature. The shepherd guards, guides, and corrects. He does not exploit. He does not coerce for personal gain. He models the conduct he expects.

This distinction is critical for cultural formation. If leaders use governance to enforce personal preferences detached from Scripture, they move toward control. If leaders refuse to enforce biblical standards to avoid discomfort, they abandon governance. Biblical leadership requires both authority and humility. Authority without humility becomes oppression. Humility without authority becomes disorder.

Governance rooted in Scripture provides objective standards. Correction is not personal retaliation. It aligns with biblical instruction. Structure is not an attempt to dominate. It is an effort to preserve clarity and faithfulness. When governance is anchored in biblical authority rather than personality, it avoids the trap of control.

Control centers leadership around itself. Governance centers leadership under Christ. Control demands submission to a person. Governance calls the congregation to submit to Scripture. Control often silences dissent without instruction. Governance explains, teaches, corrects, and invites alignment under truth.

The difference also appears in tone. Control is reactive and defensive. Governance is steady and principled. Control seeks compliance for security. Governance seeks obedience for holiness. Over time, the congregation discerns the difference. Where leadership reflects servant authority, trust strengthens. Where leadership reflects personal domination, fear, or resentment grows.

In the local church, governance must be firm yet humble, clear yet compassionate, structured yet servant-hearted. It exists to protect the flock and preserve conviction under Christ's authority. When rightly exercised, governance does not diminish spiritual vitality. It safeguards it.

Authority, Accountability, and Answerability

Authority in the local church is never autonomous. It is delegated, limited, and accountable. To understand governance rightly, leaders must understand that authority always exists alongside accountability and answerability. Authority without accountability becomes abuse. Accountability without authority becomes paralysis. Scripture binds them together.

Romans 14:12 (KJV) declares, "So then every one of us shall give account of himself to God." This principle applies universally, but it carries particular weight for those who lead. Governance decisions are not ultimately evaluated by congregational approval or numerical growth. They are evaluated before God. Every tolerance, every correction avoided, every discipline applied, every policy enacted will stand under divine review.

James 3:1 (KJV) sharpens this further: "My brethren, be not many masters, knowing that we shall receive the greater condemnation." Those who teach and lead are held to a stricter standard. Authority increases responsibility. Leadership is not merely influence; it is heightened accountability. This truth should produce sobriety in governance, not insecurity. Leaders must govern, but they must do so with awareness that their actions carry eternal consequences.

Authority in the local church is therefore answerable in two directions. It is answerable upward to God and outward to the congregation. Upward accountability reminds leaders that they steward what belongs to Christ. Outward accountability reminds leaders that they serve a body entrusted to their care. Neither direction permits isolation. Governance is not private control behind closed doors. It is visible stewardship under Scripture.

This principle also protects congregations. When leadership understands that it must answer to God, governance is tempered by humility. When leadership understands that Scripture governs its authority, it cannot justify decisions based solely on personal preference. Authority exercised under accountability builds trust. Authorities exercised without it eroding credibility.

Answerability also clarifies discipline. Correction is not a personal assertion. It is obedience to biblical instruction. Refusing to correct when Scripture requires it is not kindness. It is neglect of stewardship. Likewise, exercising authority harshly in self-defense is not strength. It is misapplication of office.

In the local church, authority must always be tethered to Scripture, shaped by humility, and exercised with awareness of final judgment. Governance that forgets accountability becomes self-protective. Governance that remembers answerability becomes faithful.

Leadership is not merely empowered. It is accountable. Every decision stands before God. That reality anchors governance in reverence rather than ego and protects culture from drifting under unchecked authority.

Chapter Three
Conviction Before Conduct

Culture in the local church does not begin with behavior. It begins with conviction. Conduct is the visible expression of what is believed, valued, and enforced. If the church attempts to regulate conduct without establishing conviction, the result will either be legalism or inconsistency. When conviction is clear and deeply rooted, conduct follows naturally through repetition and reinforcement.

This principle appears consistently throughout Scripture. Jesus teaches that behavior flows from the heart. Luke 6:45 (KJV) states, "A good man out of the good treasure of his heart bringeth forth that which is good." The heart is the source. Conduct is the result. In congregational life, this pattern multiplies across the body. Shared conviction forms shared expectations. Shared expectations form cultural patterns.

Conviction is not merely intellectual agreement with doctrine. It is belief that governs decision-making. A church may affirm the authority of the Bible while, in practice, operating under the dictates of preference or convenience. Members respond to the most visible signals rather than the stated theology. Leadership tone, tolerated speech, worship posture, and disciplinary response begin shaping culture more powerfully than the church's doctrinal statement.

For this reason, conviction must be both taught and embodied. Doctrine forms the mind, but example forms expectation. When leaders consistently demonstrate reverence, humility, clarity, and obedience to Scripture, those patterns communicate conviction more effectively than instruction alone. Conversely, when leadership behavior contradicts what is preached, the contradiction becomes instructive. Congregants quickly learn which convictions are symbolic and which are governing.

Conviction also requires repetition. Deuteronomy repeatedly instructs Israel to rehearse God's commands diligently to their children. Truth was not meant to be mentioned occasionally but embedded through continual reminder. The same principle applies within the church. Conviction grows stronger when doctrine, correction, worship, and daily conduct reinforce the same theological priorities.

When conviction weakens, conduct fragments. Without a clear governing belief, members default to personal interpretation. One group may pursue reverence while another pursues entertainment. One leader may correct while another avoids confrontation. One ministry may emphasize doctrine while another emphasizes experience. Over time, these inconsistencies produce cultural confusion. The church becomes a collection of preferences rather than a unified body.

Therefore, governance must begin at the level of conviction. Leaders must clarify what the church truly believes about holiness, authority, worship, speech, discipline, stewardship, and community. These convictions must then be reinforced consistently through teaching, policy, correction, and example. When conviction governs conduct, culture stabilizes. When conduct is addressed without conviction, culture becomes reactive and temporary.

The order is essential. Belief forms conviction. Conviction shapes conduct. Conduct repeated becomes culture. For this reason, the church must address conviction first if it desires culture that reflects biblical authority.

The Heart as the Source of Culture

The culture of a church does not originate in its programs, policies, or atmosphere. It originates in the heart. Scripture consistently teaches that outward behavior flows from inward condition. If the heart is rightly formed, conduct will eventually reflect it. If the heart is neglected, no amount of structural adjustment will produce lasting cultural health.

Proverbs 4:23 (KJV) instructs, "Keep thy heart with all diligence; for out of it are the issues of life." The heart in Scripture refers to the center of belief, desire, and moral direction. It is the governing seat of conviction. From it flow decisions, priorities, speech, and actions. What is treasured in the heart eventually becomes visible in life. This principle applies individually, but it also extends corporately within the church. A congregation's repeated behaviors reflect the collective convictions of its members and leaders.

Jesus reinforces this connection in Luke 6:45 (KJV): "A good man out of the good treasure of his heart bringeth forth that which is good… for of the abundance of the heart his mouth speaketh." The heart contains treasure, and that treasure inevitably appears in speech and conduct. The same dynamic shapes congregational culture. If reverence is treasured, reverence will appear. If entertainment is treasured, entertainment will dominate. If holiness is treasured, holiness will guide behavior. Culture reveals the treasure of the heart.

This truth explains why superficial adjustments rarely transform church culture. A church may modify lighting, alter music style, introduce new policies, or redesign gatherings, yet the underlying culture remains unchanged if the heart of the congregation remains unaddressed. Structural changes without heart formation produce temporary shifts in behavior but not lasting transformation.

For this reason, leadership must give primary attention to cultivating conviction within the heart. Teaching doctrine, modeling humility, reinforcing reverence, and correcting misalignment all contribute to shaping the congregation's internal life. As the heart is shaped, so is behavior. As behavior repeats, culture stabilizes.

It is also important to recognize that leadership hearts influence congregational hearts. Leaders set the tone. Their reverence, speech, priorities, and discipline communicate what is treasured. If leaders treat sacred things casually, the congregation will mirror that posture. If leaders approach worship, Scripture, and correction with seriousness and humility, the congregation will gradually adopt the same orientation.

Culture, therefore, is not ultimately engineered through strategy. It grows from a conviction embedded in the heart. Governance protects that conviction, but conviction itself must be formed internally through Scripture, teaching, and spiritual discipline. When the heart is guarded and rightly ordered, the resulting culture reflects biblical priorities. When the heart is neglected, culture eventually reveals the disorder within.

The heart is the fountain from which culture flows. For this reason, the formation of the heart must precede the formation of conduct if the local church is to embody a culture consistent with biblical authority.

Repetition and Formation in Deuteronomy

Biblical formation does not occur through occasional instruction. It occurs through repetition. Scripture repeatedly emphasizes that conviction must be reinforced continually if it is to shape behavior across generations. The culture of God's people has always been formed through repeated teaching, repeated remembrance, and repeated practice.

Deuteronomy 6:6–9 (KJV) provides one of the clearest instructions regarding this process:
"And these words, which I command thee this day, shall be in thine heart: And thou shalt teach them diligently unto thy children, and shalt talk of them when thou sittest in thine house, and when thou walkest by the way, and when thou liest down, and when thou risest up. And thou shalt bind them for a sign upon thine hand, and they

shall be as frontlets between thine eyes. And thou shalt write them upon the posts of thy house, and on thy gates."

This instruction demonstrates that biblical conviction was never meant to remain confined to a single moment of teaching. Truth was to permeate daily life. It was discussed at home, remembered throughout the day, and visibly reinforced in the environment. The purpose was formation. Repetition ensured that conviction became deeply embedded in both memory and conduct.

Psalm 78:5–7 (KJV) reinforces this generational responsibility: "For he established a testimony in Jacob, and appointed a law in Israel, which he commanded our fathers, that they should make them known to their children: That the generation to come might know them, even the children which should be born; who should arise and declare them to their children: That they might set their hope in God, and not forget the works of God, but keep his commandments."

Here Scripture reveals the long-term purpose of repetition. Instruction was not simply informational. It was preservational. The repeated telling of God's works and commands ensured that future generations would remember, believe, and obey. Without repetition, memory fades. When memory fades, conviction weakens. When conviction weakens, conduct changes.

The same principle applies within the local church. A congregation does not maintain biblical culture by stating convictions once in a membership class or writing them in a doctrinal statement. Convictions must be reinforced continually through preaching, discipleship, correction, worship, leadership modeling, and communal practice. What is repeated becomes remembered. What is remembered becomes believed. What is believed becomes practiced.

Repetition also creates expectation. When Scripture, reverence, humility, and obedience are reinforced consistently, members begin to recognize those behaviors as normative. They become part of the church's identity. Conversely, when repetition reinforces casual speech, entertainment-driven worship, or indifference toward holiness, those patterns become equally formative.

Deuteronomy and the Psalms reveal that formation is not accidental. It is intentional and repetitive. God instructed His people to rehearse truth continually because repetition protects conviction across time. The local church must recognize the same principle. Culture is not maintained through occasional emphasis. It is sustained through repeated reinforcement of biblical truth.

Where repetition is faithful, formation follows. Where repetition fades, culture eventually follows a different path.

Doctrine as Cultural Foundation

Culture in the local church does not begin with behavior, programming, or environment. It begins with doctrine. Doctrine establishes what the church believes about God, holiness, authority, worship, sin, and redemption. From those beliefs flow the expectations that shape conduct. If doctrine is unclear, culture becomes unstable. If doctrine is strong, culture gains a stable foundation.

Acts 2:42 (KJV) provides a clear picture of the early church: "And they continued stedfastly in the apostles' doctrine and fellowship, and in breaking of bread, and in prayers." The order here is important. Doctrine comes first. The apostles' teaching formed the theological foundation upon which fellowship, worship, and communal life were built. The early believers did not construct their community around preference or atmosphere. They organized their lives around the truths they had received.

This pattern demonstrates that doctrine shapes identity. What the church repeatedly teaches becomes the lens through which members interpret life and conduct. Doctrine teaches the congregation what to value, what to avoid, and how to respond to conflict or temptation. Without doctrinal clarity, those decisions are left to individual interpretation, and cultural unity weakens.

First Timothy 4:16 (KJV) reinforces the importance of doctrinal vigilance: “Take heed unto thyself, and unto the doctrine; continue in them: for in doing this thou shalt both save thyself, and them that hear thee.” Paul instructs Timothy to guard both personal conduct and doctrinal teaching. The two cannot be separated. Doctrine influences conduct, and conduct either confirms or undermines doctrine.

When doctrine is treated lightly, culture eventually reflects that neglect. Teaching becomes shallow. Worship becomes increasingly experience-driven. Correction becomes uncomfortable. Over time, the congregation’s identity shifts from theological conviction to emotional preference. This shift rarely occurs suddenly. It develops gradually when doctrine is no longer taken seriously.

Conversely, when doctrine remains central, culture develops depth and stability. Members understand the reasons behind behavioral expectations. Worship becomes an expression of theological truth rather than emotional stimulation alone. Discipline becomes a protection of biblical integrity rather than a personal confrontation.

Doctrine also protects unity. When beliefs are clearly articulated and consistently reinforced, the congregation shares a common framework for interpreting life and ministry. This shared framework reduces confusion and conflict. Members understand what the church stands for and what it will not compromise.

The early church recognized that doctrine was not merely informational. It was formative. The apostles’ teaching created a community shaped by shared belief and shared obedience. The same principle remains true today. Culture in the local church must rest upon doctrine as its foundation. Without doctrine, culture becomes preference. With doctrine, culture reflects conviction grounded in Scripture.

When Conviction Weakens, Conduct Fragments

When conviction weakens, culture does not remain stable. Conduct begins to fragment. Without a clear and governing conviction rooted in Scripture, individuals and ministries begin to operate according to preference, personality, or convenience. Over time, the church's shared identity erodes, and competing patterns of behavior emerge.

Revelation chapters 2 and 3 provide a sobering illustration of this process. In these letters to the seven churches, Christ evaluates not merely their doctrine but their conduct and tolerance. Some churches had preserved doctrinal clarity yet abandoned their first love. Others tolerated false teaching. Still others appeared spiritually alive but were actually dead. In each case, Christ reveals that weakened conviction produces visible cultural consequences.

The church at Ephesus had strong doctrinal discernment but had lost its first love. The church at Pergamos tolerated false teaching. The church at Thyatira allowed corrupt influence to remain within the body. The church at Sardis possessed a reputation of life but lacked true vitality. Each example demonstrates that conviction, when neglected or compromised, leads to cultural deterioration. The result is not immediate collapse but gradual fragmentation.

Second Timothy 4:3–4 (KJV) warns of the same pattern: "For the time will come when they will not endure sound doctrine; but after their own lusts shall they heap to themselves teachers, having itching ears; And they shall turn away their ears from the truth, and shall be turned unto fables." When conviction weakens, people begin to prefer messages that affirm rather than challenge. Teaching becomes shaped by demand rather than truth. Once doctrine loses authority, conduct soon follows.

This fragmentation appears in several ways within the local church. Worship priorities begin to diverge. One ministry emphasizes reverence while another prioritizes entertainment. Some leaders pursue doctrinal depth while others pursue emotional engagement. Speech becomes inconsistent. Correction becomes rare. The church begins to function less as a unified body and more as a collection of independent preferences.

Fragmentation is rarely intentional. It emerges when conviction is no longer reinforced consistently. If leaders hesitate to address doctrinal confusion, multiple interpretations develop. If correction becomes uncomfortable, tolerated behaviors expand. If holiness is rarely emphasized, casual conduct becomes normalized.

The churches in Revelation demonstrate that Christ does not evaluate congregations solely by activity or reputation. He evaluates faithfulness. He examines what is tolerated, what is corrected, and what is allowed to shape the culture of the body. Conviction must remain strong because culture always follows conviction.

When conviction is clear and consistently reinforced, conduct aligns and culture stabilizes. When conviction weakens, conduct fragments and cultural unity dissolves. The health of the local church depends not merely on activity or growth but on the strength of the convictions that govern it.

The Inevitability of Cultural Formation

Culture in the local church is inevitable. It does not wait for intentional leadership, nor does it remain neutral in the absence of clear direction. Every congregation develops patterns of behavior, expectation, and identity over time. The question is not whether culture will form, but what kind of culture will emerge from the beliefs and practices that are repeatedly reinforced.

Galatians 6:7 (KJV) establishes a governing principle that applies to both individuals and communities: “Be not deceived; God is not mocked: for whatsoever a man soweth, that shall he also reap.”

Sowing precedes harvest. Repeated actions eventually produce visible outcomes. Within the church, what is consistently taught, celebrated, tolerated, and corrected becomes the seed from which culture grows. If reverence is sown, reverence becomes visible. If casual irreverence is sown, irreverence becomes normalized. If biblical authority is reinforced, conviction strengthens. If preference is allowed to govern, conviction weakens.

This principle is reinforced in Hosea 8:7 (KJV): "For they have sown the wind, and they shall reap the whirlwind." The prophet warns that small departures from faithfulness eventually produce far greater consequences. What begins as minor compromise rarely remains minor. Cultural patterns compound over time. When truth is neglected or holiness is softened, the resulting cultural shift accelerates beyond the original decision.

These passages reveal that culture is cumulative. It is formed through repeated planting of seeds week after week. The tone of preaching, the posture of leadership, the seriousness of worship, the handling of discipline, and the expectations placed on members all contribute to the harvest that eventually appears in congregational life.

The inevitability of cultural formation also explains why passive leadership cannot preserve biblical culture. Silence becomes instruction. Tolerance becomes permission. Inconsistency becomes confusion. If governance does not intentionally reinforce biblical conviction, other forces will shape the culture instead. Social trends, generational expectations, and personal preferences will begin to fill the vacuum.

Conversely, when leaders recognize the inevitability of cultural formation, they begin to steward it intentionally. Teaching is reinforced consistently. Correction is applied when necessary. Reverence is modeled visibly. Over time, these repeated patterns create stability. Members understand what the church values because they see those values embodied repeatedly.

The local church must therefore acknowledge a simple but powerful reality: culture will form regardless of intention. The seeds are always being planted. The only question is whether those seeds align with Scripture. When the church sows conviction, it reaps faithfulness. When it sows compromise, it reaps fragmentation.

Cultural formation is inevitable because sowing is constant. Wise leadership recognizes this inevitability and governs accordingly.

PART II
Culture as a Downstream Reality

Culture in the local church does not originate at the level of atmosphere, programming, or stylistic preference. It develops from deeper governing realities that shape belief and behavior over time. For this reason, culture must be understood as downstream. It is the visible result of what leadership truly believes, what it repeatedly reinforces, and what it consistently allows.

Many churches attempt to change culture directly. They adjust the worship environment, alter language, introduce new initiatives, or attempt to generate a different emotional tone during gatherings. While these changes may affect immediate experience, they rarely produce lasting transformation. Culture does not fundamentally form at the level of atmosphere. It forms at the level of conviction and governance.

Culture emerges as people repeatedly live out the mission of the church under shared convictions. Values define the convictions the church refuses to compromise. Vision establishes long-term direction. Mission clarifies the daily work of the church. Strategy channels behavior toward that mission. Policy establishes boundaries that protect conviction. Over time, the interaction of these elements produces repeated patterns of conduct. Those patterns become culture.

Because culture is downstream, it reflects what leadership actually enforces rather than what leadership merely declares. A church may publish strong values, yet if those values are not reinforced through governance, the resulting culture will contradict them. Vision may be inspiring, but if mission and daily practice do not reinforce that direction, members will eventually follow other priorities. Culture always exposes what is truly governing the body.

For this reason, culture often reveals alignment or misalignment within leadership systems. When belief and behavior consistently correspond, the congregation develops stability and shared expectation. When stated convictions and lived behavior diverge, fragmentation begins to appear. The church may continue functioning outwardly, but the underlying culture will gradually shift away from its declared foundation.

This section examines the structural realities that shape culture beneath the surface of congregational life. The chapters that follow will explore how values establish conviction, how vision and mission reinforce daily behavior, and how governance determines what is celebrated, tolerated, and corrected within the church. These forces form the conditions from which culture emerges.

Understanding culture as a downstream reality shifts leadership focus to the correct level of responsibility. Leaders do not primarily engineer culture through atmosphere. They steward conviction, reinforce mission, and govern behavior under biblical authority. When these deeper elements align with Scripture, culture naturally stabilizes. When they are neglected, culture changes regardless of intention.

Chapter Four
Values as Governing Authority

Values function as the governing authority beneath culture. They define what a church truly believes is right, necessary, and non-negotiable. While many organizations publish value statements as aspirational language, biblical values operate differently. In the local church, values must function as binding convictions that guide leadership decisions, shape congregational expectations, and regulate behavior over time.

Values are not primarily statements on paper. They are governing beliefs that determine how leaders respond to real situations. When conflict arises, values determine whether unity or preference prevails. When correction becomes necessary, values determine whether holiness or comfort is protected. When difficult decisions must be made, values reveal what the church truly considers most important.

Because values operate at this foundational level, they function as authority within the leadership structure. They define the boundaries within which vision, mission, strategy, and policy operate. If values are unclear, every subsequent decision becomes negotiable. If values are clearly defined and consistently reinforced, they create stability throughout the entire leadership system.

In the local church, biblical values must originate from Scripture rather than cultural trends or organizational fashion. Scripture establishes the moral and theological framework that defines holiness, humility, reverence, unity, truthfulness, and stewardship. These principles become the convictions that guide leadership and shape congregational life. When values remain rooted in biblical authority, the church retains clarity even when external pressures attempt to redefine its priorities.

Values also reveal what leadership truly believes. Congregations observe not only what leaders teach but also what they protect and tolerate. When leaders consistently reinforce biblical convictions, those convictions become embedded in the church's culture. When leaders hesitate to enforce them, the congregation gradually learns that those values are optional.

This is why values must function as governing authority rather than inspirational language. They establish the standards that determine acceptable conduct within the body. They guide leadership decisions during moments of uncertainty. They protect the church from drifting toward preferences that contradict biblical teaching.

Within the LCSM10 framework, values form the deepest layer of leadership alignment. Vision provides direction, mission defines activity, strategy organizes action, and policy establishes guardrails. Yet all of these depend upon the governing authority of values. If values are compromised, every other component becomes unstable.

For this reason, the health of church culture depends heavily on whether values truly govern the body. When values remain clear, reinforced, and rooted in Scripture, culture reflects conviction rather than preference. When values become symbolic rather than governing, culture inevitably shifts toward whatever influence is strongest at the moment. Values stand at the headwaters of culture. They do not merely describe what a church hopes to become. They govern what the church actually becomes.

Conviction as the Root System

Conviction functions as the root system beneath the life of the church. Just as roots anchor a tree and supply the nourishment that sustains growth, conviction anchors a congregation and supplies the beliefs that sustain its culture. What is rooted deeply will eventually become visible externally. What lacks root structure will struggle to endure when pressure arises.

Psalm 1:1–3 (KJV) provides a powerful image of this reality. The righteous person is described as one whose delight is in the law of the Lord and who meditates upon it continually. The result is a life "like a tree planted by the rivers of water, that bringeth forth his fruit in his season." The fruit is visible, but it is not the starting point. It is the result of deep-rooting. The tree draws life from a steady source, and because its roots are secure, its growth becomes stable and productive.

The same principle applies to the local church's culture. The visible behaviors of a congregation, its reverence, speech, worship posture, discipline, and unity, are the fruit. Beneath that fruit lies conviction. Conviction draws nourishment from Scripture and is strengthened through teaching, repetition, and faithful leadership. When conviction is deeply rooted, the resulting conduct remains stable even in the face of conflict or cultural pressure.

Colossians 2:6–7 (KJV) reinforces this imagery: "As ye have therefore received Christ Jesus the Lord, so walk ye in him: rooted and built up in him, and stablished in the faith." The language again begins beneath the surface. Believers are rooted before they are built up. Stability grows from depth. Faith that is firmly rooted produces conduct that reflects that faith in daily life.

In the context of the local church, conviction functions as this root system for culture. Leaders may address behavior directly, but lasting transformation requires strengthening the convictions beneath that behavior. When members understand why holiness matters, why reverence matters, why truth matters, and why unity matters, those beliefs begin to guide their choices without constant external correction.

Conversely, when conviction remains shallow, cultural instability soon follows. The church may display outward vitality for a time, but without deep roots, behavior will shift quickly when pressure or preference challenges biblical standards. Conviction that is weak cannot sustain a culture of faithfulness.

For this reason, leadership must prioritize cultivating conviction. Teaching Scripture, reinforcing doctrine, modeling obedience, and correcting misalignment all contribute to strengthening the church's root system. As conviction deepens, conduct stabilizes. As conduct stabilizes, culture becomes consistent.

Healthy culture grows from rooted conviction. The deeper the roots extend into biblical truth, the stronger the church's visible life will become.

What Leadership Truly Believes

The culture of a church ultimately reveals what its leaders truly believe. While sermons, mission statements, and public language may describe certain convictions, the consistent behavior of leadership exposes which beliefs actually govern the church. Congregations watch their leaders closely, and over time, they learn which standards are real and which are merely spoken.

Jesus addressed this principle directly in Matthew 12:34 (KJV): "For out of the abundance of the heart the mouth speaketh." Words and actions flow from what is already present within the heart. Leadership speech, priorities, and reactions reveal internal conviction. If reverence, holiness, and truth truly live within the heart of leadership, those convictions will consistently appear in teaching, correction, and example.

Because of this reality, leaders' personal conduct carries enormous cultural weight. Leaders do not only teach doctrine. They demonstrate how that doctrine is lived. Their tone, humility, speech, discipline, and spiritual seriousness shape the congregation's expectations. Over time, people begin to mirror what they repeatedly observe.

The apostle Paul emphasized this responsibility in 1 Timothy 4:12 (KJV): “Be thou an example of the believers, in word, in conversation, in charity, in spirit, in faith, in purity.” Leadership example functions as instruction. The life of the leader becomes a living demonstration of the standards that should guide the church.

This means culture cannot be separated from leadership character. If leaders treat sacred things casually, the congregation will eventually do the same. If leaders guard doctrine carefully, the church will learn to value truth. If leaders demonstrate humility and reverence before God, those traits begin to form within the body as well.

The opposite is also true. When leaders preach convictions they do not consistently live, congregations quickly detect the contradiction. Over time, this can lead to confusion or cynicism. Members may still hear the message, but they learn that the stated standard does not truly govern behavior. When this gap widens, culture begins to weaken.

Healthy church culture requires leadership whose convictions are both spoken and demonstrated. Teaching must be reinforced through consistent conduct. The values leaders proclaim must appear in their daily decisions and interactions.

In this way, leadership belief becomes visible through leadership behavior. What leaders truly believe will always become visible in how they live, how they lead, and what they choose to protect within the church.

Written Values Versus Enforced Values

Many churches can clearly articulate their values. They appear on websites, in membership materials, in mission documents, and in leadership presentations. Words such as love, truth, discipleship, unity, and holiness are commonly written and publicly affirmed. Yet the presence of written values does not automatically produce a culture shaped by those values.

The real question is whether those values are enforced.

Scripture warns about the danger of honoring God with words while living differently in practice. Isaiah 29:13 (KJV) records the Lord's rebuke: "This people draw near me with their mouth, and with their lips do honour me, but have removed their heart far from me." The problem was not the language. The problem was the separation between confession and conduct. What was spoken publicly did not govern how people actually lived.

This same danger exists within the life of the church. Values may be written clearly, but if leadership does not reinforce them through decision-making, correction, and example, those values slowly become symbolic rather than governing. The congregation eventually learns that the values are aspirational statements rather than binding convictions.

James addresses this issue directly in James 1:22 (KJV): "But be ye doers of the word, and not hearers only, deceiving your own selves." Biblical truth is not intended to remain theoretical. It must move from declaration into action. When truth is heard but not practiced, self-deception develops.

The same principle applies to organizational values. Written values communicate intention. Enforced values create culture. What leadership corrects, protects, and reinforces determines which values actually govern the church.

For example, a church may declare that unity is one of its values. Yet if gossip is tolerated without correction, the real message becomes clear. The written value exists, but the enforced value is different. Similarly, a church may proclaim holiness, but if casual attitudes toward sin are ignored, the congregation gradually learns that holiness is not truly expected.

Over time, enforced values always outweigh written values. Congregations observe leadership behavior, leadership decisions, and leadership silence. From those signals, they determine what the church truly believes matters.

For this reason, leadership must ensure that written values are reinforced through consistent practice. Teaching must be accompanied by correction. Standards must be protected. Decisions must align with the convictions the church claims to hold.

When written values and enforced values remain aligned, trust develops and culture stabilizes. When they diverge, confusion grows, and the credibility of leadership weakens. Values only become real when they are consistently lived and guarded within the life of the church.

Alignment Between Confession and Practice

Healthy church culture requires alignment between what is confessed and how people actually live. The message proclaimed by the church must be reflected in the conduct of its leaders and congregation. When confession and practice remain consistent, the church presents a unified testimony. When they diverge, credibility begins to weaken.

The apostle Paul addressed this principle in Philippians 1:27 (KJV): "Only let your conversation be as it becometh the gospel of Christ." The word "conversation" refers to one's manner of life. Paul's instruction was not simply about verbal proclamation. The life of the believer was to match the message of the gospel. Conduct was expected to reflect the truth being preached.

This same expectation applies to the life of the local church. Doctrine, teaching, and public confession form the theological identity of the congregation. Yet that identity must also manifest in the body's daily life. Worship posture, speech, relationships, leadership conduct, and congregational behavior all communicate whether the church truly lives what it proclaims.

Scripture also warns about the danger of claiming knowledge of God while living contrary to His commands. 1 John 2:4 (KJV) states, “He that saith, I know him, and keepeth not his commandments, is a liar, and the truth is not in him.” This passage highlights the seriousness of misalignment between confession and conduct. Genuine belief reveals itself through obedience.

Within the local church, alignment between confession and practice produces clarity. Members understand what the church believes because they see those convictions demonstrated consistently. Leaders reinforce the same message through both teaching and example. Over time, this consistency builds trust and strengthens unity.

However, when practice contradicts confession, confusion quickly spreads. If a church teaches reverence but behaves casually toward sacred things, the congregation receives mixed signals. If holiness is preached but rarely enforced, members begin to question whether those standards truly matter. Misalignment gradually weakens both leadership authority and congregational confidence.

Alignment requires deliberate attention. Leaders must ensure that decisions, behavior, and correction reflect the convictions the church publicly affirms. Teaching must be reinforced through visible obedience. The values declared from the pulpit must also guide the everyday life of the body.

When confession and practice remain aligned, the church becomes a living testimony of the gospel it proclaims. The message of Christ is not only spoken. It is demonstrated through the congregation's consistent life.

The Cost of Unenforced Conviction

Convictions that are not enforced gradually lose their authority. A church may clearly state what it believes, but when those convictions are not protected through leadership decisions and correction, the congregation eventually learns that those standards are optional. Over time, the gap between belief and behavior widens, and the church's culture begins to shift.

Scripture provides several warnings about the consequences of tolerated compromise. In Revelation 2:20 (KJV), the Lord rebukes the church at Thyatira: "Notwithstanding I have a few things against thee, because thou sufferest that woman Jezebel... to teach and to seduce my servants." The issue was not only false teaching itself but the church's willingness to allow it to remain. Toleration of error became the pathway through which corruption entered the body.

This principle appears again in 1 Corinthians 5:6 (KJV): "Know ye not that a little leaven leaveneth the whole lump?" Small compromises rarely remain small. When unhealthy behavior, false doctrine, or destructive attitudes are left uncorrected, they begin to influence the broader culture of the church. What begins as isolated conduct slowly spreads through imitation and acceptance.

Unenforced conviction carries a measurable cost. First, it weakens leadership credibility. When leaders state a conviction but fail to act when that conviction is violated, the congregation recognizes the inconsistency. Members may continue to hear the teaching, but they begin to question whether the standard truly matters.

Second, unenforced conviction gradually reshapes expectations within the congregation. Behaviors that were once considered inappropriate slowly become normalized. New members observe the church's existing conduct and assume it reflects the accepted culture.

Third, the church begins to lose its spiritual distinctiveness. Biblical standards are replaced by cultural preferences, and the boundaries that once protected the life of the body become less clear. Without reinforcement, conviction slowly fades into tradition rather than active belief.

For this reason, leadership must recognize that conviction without reinforcement cannot sustain a healthy church culture. Teaching must be supported by correction, and standards must be protected when they are challenged. Discipline, when practiced with humility and restoration in mind, serves to preserve the integrity of the church rather than harm it.

When convictions are consistently reinforced, they remain living standards within the body. When they are ignored, they gradually dissolve. The cost of unenforced conviction is not simply inconsistency. It is the slow transformation of the church's culture away from the beliefs it once claimed to hold.

Chapter Five
Vision and Mission as Cultural Reinforcement

Values establish the church's governing convictions, but vision and mission determine how those convictions are expressed in daily life. While values answer the question of what the church believes, vision and mission clarify where the church is going and what it is committed to doing. Together, they reinforce the beliefs that shape culture and guide behavior within the body.

Vision provides directional clarity. It describes the future that the church believes God is calling it to pursue. When a church clearly understands its direction, leadership decisions, ministry priorities, and congregational energy begin to move in a unified direction. Vision, therefore, influences culture by focusing attention and shaping expectations about what matters most.

Mission, by contrast, defines the ongoing work of the church. It describes the primary activities through which the church fulfills its calling. Preaching the gospel, making disciples, serving the community, and strengthening believers are not abstract ideals. They become repeated actions that reinforce the church's convictions through consistent practice.

Because culture forms through repetition, mission plays a particularly powerful role in shaping congregational life. What the church consistently does eventually becomes what the church naturally values. Ministries that receive attention, resources, and leadership support begin to influence the attitudes and behavior of the congregation.

When vision and mission align with biblical convictions, they reinforce the church's values. Leaders make decisions that support the vision and the mission's work. Members observe these priorities and begin to organize their own participation around them. Over time, the church's culture begins to reflect the convictions expressed through these repeated activities.

However, when vision and mission lack clarity, culture becomes unstable. Ministries compete for attention, priorities shift frequently, and the congregation receives mixed signals about what the church is truly committed to accomplishing. Without clear direction and defined activity, cultural formation becomes inconsistent.

Within the LCSM10 framework, vision and mission operate downstream from values but upstream from culture. Values define conviction, vision establishes direction, and mission guides action. As these elements remain aligned, culture becomes the visible reflection of leadership clarity and congregational commitment.

For this reason, vision and mission should never exist as isolated statements. They must actively reinforce the convictions that define the church. When leadership consistently aligns direction and activity with biblical values, culture gradually stabilizes around those shared commitments.

Direction Shapes Behavior

The direction a church pursues inevitably shapes its people's behavior. When leadership clearly communicates where the church is going and why that direction matters, members begin to organize their participation around that shared purpose. Over time, the direction established by vision influences decisions, priorities, and everyday conduct within the congregation.

Proverbs 29:18 (KJV) highlights the importance of direction in spiritual life: “Where there is no vision, the people perish: but he that keepeth the law, happy is he.” Vision provides clarity, helping prevent confusion and disorder. Without clear direction, people begin to follow their own preferences and interpretations, resulting in fragmentation rather than unity.

In the life of the local church, vision helps guide the collective focus of the body. When the church understands its purpose, ministry efforts become coordinated rather than scattered. Members begin to see how their gifts and participation contribute to a larger work. This clarity shapes how people serve, how they prioritize their time, and how they understand their role within the church community.

Hebrews 12:1–2 (KJV) offers a similar image of directed focus in the Christian life: “Let us run with patience the race that is set before us, looking unto Jesus the author and finisher of our faith.” The Christian life is described as a race with a defined course. Believers are called to remove distractions and keep their attention fixed on Christ. Direction produces discipline, perseverance, and intentional conduct.

This same principle applies to congregational life. When the church focuses on a clear biblical vision, behavior begins to align with that vision. Ministries develop in that direction, leaders reinforce it through their decisions, and members adopt attitudes that support the church's mission.

Without clear direction, behavior becomes reactive rather than purposeful. Individuals pursue personal interests rather than shared priorities. Ministries multiply without coordination, and the church's culture is shaped by preference rather than conviction.

For this reason, leadership must provide consistent direction that aligns with biblical teaching. Vision does more than describe the future of the church. It shapes the congregation's present behavior by clarifying what the church is striving to accomplish together.

When direction remains clear and centered on Christ, behavior within the church begins to reflect that focus. Members run the same race, pursue the same purpose, and reinforce a culture that moves the church forward in unity and faithfulness.

Mission as Daily Repetition

Mission shapes culture through repetition. While vision describes the direction of the church, mission defines the work the church repeatedly performs. What a congregation practices consistently becomes what it naturally values. Over time, these repeated actions form habits that, in turn, shape the church's culture.

Jesus established the central mission of the church in Matthew 28:19–20 (KJV): "Go ye therefore, and teach all nations, baptizing them in the name of the Father, and of the Son, and of the Holy Ghost: Teaching them to observe all things whatsoever I have commanded you." The Great Commission is not a one-time event. It is an ongoing assignment that requires continual action. Teaching, baptizing, and discipling are activities that must be repeated generation after generation.

Because mission involves repeated practice, it gradually forms the character of the church. When evangelism, discipleship, and teaching remain central to church life, members begin to adopt those priorities personally. The mission becomes embedded in the daily rhythms of ministry and congregational participation.

Acts 2:42 (KJV) provides an example of this principle in the early church: "And they continued stedfastly in the apostles' doctrine and fellowship, and in breaking of bread, and in prayers." These believers practiced certain activities consistently. Doctrine, fellowship, worship, and prayer were not occasional events but regular patterns of life within the church. Through repetition, these practices formed the congregation's spiritual culture.

This principle remains true for the local church today. The ministries that receive regular attention and participation shape the congregation's spiritual habits. If discipleship is repeated faithfully, believers grow in understanding. If prayer is practiced regularly, dependence upon God deepens. If fellowship is nurtured consistently, unity strengthens.

However, if the mission becomes unclear or inconsistent, repetition weakens. Programs may change frequently, priorities shift, and members struggle to understand how they should participate in the life of the church. Without steady repetition of meaningful mission activity, cultural formation becomes unstable.

For this reason, the mission must be reinforced through consistent practice. Leaders must ensure that the church's central work remains visible and active. Teaching, discipleship, worship, and service must be practiced regularly so that the congregation experiences the mission rather than merely hearing about it.

When mission becomes the repeated rhythm of church life, culture begins to reflect those practices. The congregation learns through participation, and over time, the habits formed by mission become the character of the church itself.

Strategy as Behavioral Channel

Strategy functions as the channel through which mission becomes organized action. While vision establishes direction and mission defines the work of the church, strategy determines how that work will be carried out in a practical and coordinated way. Without strategy, good intentions often remain unorganized, and ministry efforts become scattered rather than focused.

In the life of the church, strategy guides behavior by providing structure for how people participate in the mission. It determines how discipleship is organized, how outreach is conducted, how ministries are prioritized, and how resources are allocated. Strategy shapes the rhythms and habits that members experience as they engage in the life of the congregation.

Jesus illustrated the importance of thoughtful planning in Luke 14:28–30 (KJV): “For which of you, intending to build a tower, sitteth not down first, and counteth the cost, whether he have sufficient to finish it?” The passage emphasizes the necessity of deliberate preparation before beginning a significant undertaking. Planning ensures that effort is directed wisely and that the intended work can be completed.

This principle applies directly to the ministry of the church. Vision and mission may clearly describe what the church desires to accomplish, but strategy determines whether those goals can be pursued effectively. When leaders intentionally organize ministry efforts, the congregation receives clear pathways for participation and service.

Strategy also helps prevent confusion and duplication of effort. Without a coordinated plan, ministries may compete for attention or unintentionally work against one another. A clear strategy channels energy toward common priorities and allows the church to move forward with unity and purpose.

Because strategy influences how the mission is practiced, it also shapes behavior within the church. The systems and structures leadership establishes become the patterns through which members engage with the life of the congregation. Over time, those patterns reinforce the church's cultural expectations.

For this reason, strategy should remain aligned with the church's convictions and mission. Planning must serve the biblical priorities that define the church’s purpose. When strategy supports those priorities, it becomes a healthy channel through which mission activity flows, and culture is strengthened through consistent practice.

Policy as Cultural Guardrail

Policy serves as the guardrail that protects the church's mission and culture. While values establish conviction, vision sets direction, mission defines activity, and strategy organizes action, policy provides the boundaries that preserve alignment. Without clear guardrails, even well-intentioned ministries can slowly drift away from the convictions that originally guided them.

Policies establish consistent expectations for how decisions are made and how responsibilities are carried out. They define procedures for leadership conduct, financial stewardship, ministry oversight, and accountability. These structures help prevent confusion and ensure that the church's practices remain aligned with its stated beliefs.

The importance of protective structure appears throughout Scripture. In Nehemiah 4:9 (KJV), the people rebuilding Jerusalem faced constant opposition. The response was both spiritual and practical: "Nevertheless we made our prayer unto our God, and set a watch against them day and night." Prayer expressed dependence on God, while the watch protected the work. Both were necessary to maintain the mission's progress.

Similarly, Titus 1:5 (KJV) shows the importance of ordered leadership within the church: "For this cause left I thee in Crete, that thou shouldest set in order the things that are wanting, and ordain elders in every city." Paul instructed Titus to establish structure so that the life of the church would remain stable and accountable. Order protected the ministry's integrity.

Policy serves a similar purpose in modern church governance. It does not replace spiritual leadership or the work of the Holy Spirit. Rather, it creates a framework that helps leaders faithfully steward their responsibilities. Guardrails ensure that decisions remain consistent with the church's convictions and mission.

Without such boundaries, cultural shifts can occur gradually and without clear awareness. Practices that were once exceptions may slowly become normalized. Ministries may drift toward preferences that conflict with biblical teaching. Clear policies help prevent this erosion by establishing standards that guide behavior and decision-making.

When policy is aligned with biblical convictions, it reinforces the culture the church seeks to maintain. Leaders understand their responsibilities, members recognize the expectations of participation, and the church's mission remains protected from unnecessary confusion or compromise.

Alignment as Cultural Stability

Cultural stability in the local church depends on alignment. When values, vision, mission, strategy, and policy support one another, the church operates with clarity and unity. Members understand what the church believes, where it is going, and how they participate in the work. This alignment produces consistency in behavior and reinforces the culture the church seeks to cultivate.

Ephesians 4:1–3 (KJV) emphasizes this principle of unity and ordered life within the body of Christ: "I therefore, the prisoner of the Lord, beseech you that ye walk worthy of the vocation wherewith ye are called, With all lowliness and meekness, with longsuffering, forbearing one another in love; Endeavouring to keep the unity of the Spirit in the bond of peace." Paul calls believers to live in a manner worthy of their calling and to work intentionally toward unity. Such unity is sustained when the life of the church moves in the same direction.

Alignment ensures that leadership language and leadership action remain consistent. Values inform the church's vision. Vision guides the mission. Mission is carried out through strategy. Policy protects the integrity of those efforts. When these elements remain connected, the church avoids confusion and maintains a stable cultural environment.

Without alignment, instability begins to appear. Ministries may pursue different priorities, leaders may send mixed signals through their decisions, and the congregation may struggle to understand what truly matters. Over time, these inconsistencies weaken unity and allow culture to be shaped by preference rather than conviction.

For this reason, alignment must be continually reinforced by leadership. Decisions, ministries, and policies must consistently reflect the convictions the church claims to hold. When alignment is maintained, the church develops a culture marked by unity, clarity, and shared purpose. The congregation moves forward together, reinforcing the same convictions through their collective life and ministry.

Chapter Six
The Enforcement Principle

Values, vision, and mission establish the convictions, direction, and work of the church. However, the presence of these statements alone does not ensure that they shape the congregation's life. Cultural formation requires more than declaration. It requires consistent reinforcement through leadership action. The Enforcement Principle recognizes that beliefs become visible in behavior only when leadership consistently upholds the convictions it claims to hold.

In the life of the church, enforcement does not refer to authoritarian control or harsh discipline. Rather, it describes the leadership's responsibility to protect the integrity of the church's convictions through consistent guidance and correction. Leaders reinforce what is right, address what is harmful, and maintain alignment between the church's stated beliefs and its actual practices. Without this stewardship, even the most carefully written values and mission statements gradually lose their influence.

Scripture repeatedly affirms the responsibility of leadership to guard the integrity of the community of faith. Hebrews 13:17 (KJV) instructs believers to respect the spiritual authority entrusted to church leaders: "Obey them that have the rule over you, and submit yourselves: for they watch for your souls, as they that must give account." The passage reminds the church that leadership involves accountability before God for the spiritual health of the congregation. Such responsibility requires leaders to actively guide and protect the life of the church.

The Enforcement Principle, therefore, recognizes that leadership inevitably shapes culture through what it permits and what it corrects. Practices that are consistently encouraged become habits within the congregation. Behaviors that are ignored or tolerated gradually become accepted patterns of life. Over time, these patterns shape the church's culture. For this reason, leadership decisions about reinforcement and correction have a lasting influence on the spiritual character of the congregation.

Throughout Scripture, spiritual leaders were called not only to teach truth but also to guard it. In Titus 1:9 (KJV), church leaders are instructed to hold firmly to sound doctrine so that they may both encourage believers and refute those who oppose it. Teaching alone was not considered sufficient. Leaders were also responsible for preserving the integrity of the teaching by addressing errors when they appeared.

This principle remains essential for the local church today. If leaders fail to reinforce the convictions they proclaim, the church gradually drifts. Members observe the gap between what is said and what is practiced. Over time, this inconsistency weakens trust, confuses priorities, and allows culture to form around convenience rather than conviction.

By contrast, when leadership consistently reinforces the church's values, vision, and mission, cultural clarity develops. Members understand what the church believes and how those beliefs are expressed in daily life. The congregation begins to reflect those convictions through shared habits, expectations, and patterns of ministry.

The Enforcement Principle reminds leaders that culture is not shaped solely by statements. Culture is shaped by what leadership consistently reinforces. When leaders steward their authority with humility, wisdom, and biblical conviction, they help preserve the integrity of the church's mission and protect the spiritual health of the congregation.

Culture Is Formed by What Is Celebrated

Culture within the church is shaped not only by what leaders teach, but also by what leaders celebrate. When certain behaviors, attitudes, or ministries receive public encouragement and recognition, they begin to signal to the congregation what is valued. Over time, what is celebrated becomes what is repeated, and what is repeated gradually forms the culture of the church.

Celebration functions as a powerful form of reinforcement. When leaders affirm actions that reflect the church's values and mission, they communicate that these behaviors represent the direction the congregation should pursue. Members observe which activities receive attention, gratitude, and support. These signals influence how individuals choose to serve, how ministries develop, and how the church expresses its shared convictions.

Scripture recognizes the role of encouragement in reinforcing righteous behavior. Romans 13:3 (KJV) explains that governing authorities exist to affirm what is right: "For rulers are not a terror to good works, but to the evil. Wilt thou then not be afraid of the power? do that which is good, and thou shalt have praise of the same." While the passage addresses civil authority, the principle applies broadly to leadership. When good actions receive praise and recognition, they are strengthened and repeated.

This principle also appears in the instructions given to believers regarding their thoughts and attention. Philippians 4:8 (KJV) instructs the church to focus on what reflects godly character: "Whatsoever things are true, whatsoever things are honest, whatsoever things are just, whatsoever things are pure, whatsoever things are lovely, whatsoever things are of good report; if there be any virtue, and if there be any praise, think on these things." By directing attention toward what is virtuous and praiseworthy, the church reinforces the behaviors and attitudes that reflect its convictions.

In congregational life, this means that the ministries, attitudes, and actions that receive encouragement from leadership gradually influence the direction of the church. When leaders consistently celebrate faithfulness, service, discipleship, generosity, and humility, those qualities begin to shape the congregation's expectations. Members recognize what reflects the church's mission and begin to align their participation with those priorities.

However, if celebration becomes disconnected from the church's convictions and mission, confusion begins to develop. Activities that may be impressive but not spiritually formative can begin to dominate attention. Over time, the congregation may begin to value visibility, recognition, or personal achievement more than faithfulness and spiritual growth.

For this reason, leadership must exercise wisdom in what it chooses to highlight and celebrate. Recognition should reinforce the convictions and mission that define the church. When celebration aligns with biblical values, it strengthens the culture the church seeks to cultivate and encourages members to participate in the body's shared work.

Through intentional encouragement, leadership reinforces the behaviors that reflect the heart of the church. As those behaviors are repeated and celebrated, they gradually shape the congregation's culture and strengthen its unity in mission.

Culture Is Formed by What Is Tolerated

While culture is strengthened by what leadership celebrates, it is also shaped by what leadership tolerates. Behaviors, attitudes, and practices that are allowed to continue without correction gradually become accepted as normal within the life of the church. Over time, tolerance of harmful patterns can influence the direction of the congregation just as powerfully as encouragement of healthy ones.

Leadership inevitably communicates standards through its response to conduct within the community. When actions that contradict the church's convictions or mission are ignored, members may assume they are acceptable. Even when leadership has clearly stated values, those values lose their influence if practices that conflict with them remain unaddressed.

The letters to the churches in Revelation illustrate the seriousness of this principle. In Revelation 2:14–20 (KJV), Christ rebukes several congregations not only for false teaching but also for their willingness to tolerate it. The church in Pergamos is warned because it allowed those who held corrupt teaching to remain among them. The church in Thyatira receives a similar rebuke for permitting a false prophetess to lead believers into deception. In both cases, the issue was not simply the presence of error but the church's willingness to allow that error to continue without correction.

These passages demonstrate that tolerance of harmful influences can gradually reshape a congregation's spiritual environment. When practices that contradict biblical teaching remain unchallenged, they begin to shape the church's beliefs, behavior, and expectations. What begins as a small compromise can slowly alter the culture of the entire community.

For this reason, leadership must remain attentive to the congregation's health. Protecting the spiritual integrity of the church sometimes requires addressing issues that threaten unity, doctrine, or conduct. Such correction should always be exercised with humility, wisdom, and a desire for restoration rather than condemnation. Nevertheless, faithful leadership cannot ignore practices that undermine the church's convictions.

When harmful behaviors are addressed with clarity and grace, the church preserves the integrity of its culture. Members gain confidence that the convictions of the church are more than words.

They recognize that the church's leadership is committed to protecting the spiritual health of the congregation.

The Enforcement Principle reminds leaders that culture is never neutral. It is continually shaped by the behaviors that are encouraged and those that are permitted to continue. By guarding both what is celebrated and what is tolerated, leadership helps preserve a culture that reflects the truth and mission entrusted to the church.

Culture Is Formed by What Is Corrected

Correction also plays an essential role in shaping the church's culture. While celebration reinforces healthy behavior and tolerance influences what becomes accepted, correction provides the means by which the church preserves its convictions and restores individuals who have wandered from them. Through wise and consistent correction, leadership helps maintain the integrity of the congregation and protect the unity of the body.

In every community, mistakes, misunderstandings, and failures occur. The presence of these challenges does not necessarily weaken the church. What matters is how they are addressed. When harmful behavior is corrected with clarity and humility, the church demonstrates its commitment to truth and restoration. When correction is ignored or avoided, confusion and division often increase.

Jesus established a clear pattern for correction among believers in Matthew 18:15–17 (KJV): "Moreover if thy brother shall trespass against thee, go and tell him his fault between thee and him alone." Christ instructs believers to approach correction with measured restraint and in a restorative manner. The process begins privately, allowing for repentance and reconciliation without unnecessary exposure. If the matter remains unresolved, additional witnesses may be called, and the church may address the issue if necessary. The goal of this process is not punishment but restoration and the preservation of unity within the body.

The apostle Paul also emphasizes the restorative nature of correction in Galatians 6:1 (KJV): “Brethren, if a man be overtaken in a fault, ye which are spiritual, restore such an one in the spirit of meekness; considering thyself, lest thou also be tempted.” Correction must be carried out with humility and compassion. Those who address wrongdoing must remember their own need for grace and approach others with gentleness and care.

When correction is practiced according to these biblical principles, the church's culture reflects both truth and grace. Members understand that the church is committed to holiness while also extending compassion toward those who struggle. Restoration becomes possible because correction is guided by love rather than condemnation.

Correction also reinforces accountability within the congregation. When leaders and members address harmful behavior with wisdom and patience, the church learns that convictions are not merely theoretical. They are lived out through consistent actions that protect the community's health.

Over time, these patterns shape the congregation's expectations. Members recognize that faithfulness, humility, and repentance are valued within the church. They also understand that harmful behavior will be addressed in a manner that seeks restoration rather than humiliation.

Through this process, correction becomes a vital part of cultural formation. It protects the unity of the church, restores individuals to fellowship, and reinforces the convictions that define the congregation's mission.

Crisis as Cultural Exposure

Crisis often reveals a church's true culture more clearly than ordinary circumstances. During seasons of stability, weaknesses within a congregation may remain hidden beneath routine activity and familiar patterns of ministry. However, when pressure, conflict, or uncertainty arises, the church's underlying convictions and habits quickly become visible. Crisis does not create culture. It exposes the culture that already exists.

Moments of difficulty reveal what the congregation truly believes about God, leadership, and the church's mission. When faith and unity are deeply rooted, members respond to challenges with prayer, patience, and trust in the Lord. When those convictions are weak or uncertain, fear, frustration, and division often surface. The reactions that emerge during a crisis reveal the patterns that have been forming beneath the surface over time.

The disciples experienced such a moment during the storm on the Sea of Galilee. Mark 4:37–40 (KJV) describes how a violent storm arose while Jesus and His disciples were crossing the water: "And there arose a great storm of wind, and the waves beat into the ship, so that it was now full." In their fear, the disciples awakened Jesus, asking whether He cared that they were perishing. After calming the storm, Jesus asked them, "Why are ye so fearful? how is it that ye have no faith?" The crisis exposed the gap between what the disciples had witnessed and the faith they had yet to develop fully.

The account of the golden calf in Exodus 32 provides another example of crisis revealing the condition of the people. While Moses remained on Mount Sinai receiving the law, the people quickly turned to idolatry. The pressure of uncertainty exposed a lack of trust and spiritual stability among the Israelites. Their actions revealed that their hearts had not yet fully embraced the covenant they had received.

These biblical examples demonstrate that a crisis often brings hidden cultural patterns to the surface. Moments of difficulty reveal whether a congregation is guided by faith or fear, by unity or division, by conviction or by preference. What appears during a crisis is usually the result of habits and attitudes that have developed gradually over time.

For this reason, crises can serve as important moments of evaluation for church leadership. Instead of viewing difficulty only as a disruption, leaders can also recognize it as an opportunity to observe the deeper condition of the congregation. The reactions that emerge during challenging moments reveal where convictions are strong and where further teaching, encouragement, or correction may be needed.

Healthy leadership responds to a crisis with both spiritual dependence and thoughtful reflection. Prayer, humility, and trust in God remain essential. At the same time, leaders can learn from what a crisis reveals about the church's culture. The patterns revealed in these moments often point to areas where the church's values, vision, and mission need reinforcement.

When leaders respond wisely, a crisis can become a moment of cultural strengthening rather than cultural collapse. The church can grow in maturity, deepen its reliance upon God, and renew its commitment to the convictions that guide its mission. In this way, crisis does not define the church's culture, but it often reveals the culture that leadership must continue to shape and protect.

Weak Governance and Predictable Consequences

A healthy culture within the church depends upon faithful leadership. When governance is strong, convictions remain clear, priorities remain aligned, and the congregation moves forward with unity and purpose. When governance becomes weak or inconsistent, the consequences are often predictable. Confusion increases, priorities shift, and the congregation's spiritual health gradually declines.

Weak governance does not always appear suddenly or dramatically. More often, it develops slowly as leadership becomes hesitant to reinforce convictions, unwilling to address harmful behavior, or unclear about the church's direction. Over time, the absence of consistent leadership allows competing priorities and personal preferences to influence the life of the congregation.

Scripture offers a sobering warning about the consequences of neglected leadership responsibility. In Ezekiel 34:2–6 (KJV), the Lord rebukes the shepherds of Israel for failing to care for the people entrusted to them: "Woe be to the shepherds of Israel that do feed themselves! should not the shepherds feed the flocks?" Instead of protecting and guiding the people, these leaders neglected their duties and pursued their own interests. As a result, the flock became scattered and vulnerable.

The passage continues by describing the condition of the people: "My sheep wandered through all the mountains, and upon every high hill: yea, my flock was scattered upon all the face of the earth, and none did search or seek after them." Without faithful shepherds, the people lacked protection, direction, and care. The failure of leadership created a predictable outcome: disorder and vulnerability within the community.

This principle applies directly to the governance of the local church. When leadership fails to reinforce the church's convictions, the congregation's culture becomes unstable. Ministries may drift away from the mission, doctrinal clarity may weaken, and the congregation may struggle to understand the church's direction.

Strong governance, by contrast, protects the life of the church. Leaders who faithfully uphold biblical convictions guide the congregation with clarity and integrity. They encourage healthy ministry, address harmful patterns when necessary, and maintain alignment among the church's values, vision, and mission.

The Enforcement Principle reminds leaders that governance carries significant responsibility. Leadership decisions influence the spiritual environment of the congregation and the direction of its ministry. When leaders steward their responsibilities faithfully, they help preserve the church's unity, mission, and cultural health.

For this reason, the church must view governance not as an administrative burden but as spiritual stewardship. Faithful leadership protects the flock, strengthens the mission, and ensures that the church's culture reflects the convictions that define its calling.

PART III
Visible Signals That Form Church Culture

Culture within the church is rarely shaped solely by written statements. While values, vision, and mission establish the convictions, direction, and work of the congregation, culture ultimately becomes visible through the patterns of behavior that develop within the life of the church. These patterns emerge through everyday actions, leadership decisions, and the signals that members observe and respond to over time.

Members of a congregation continually interpret what the church truly values by watching what is emphasized, what is permitted, and how leadership responds to both success and failure. These visible signals communicate expectations about participation, priorities, and conduct. Through repetition, they gradually form the habits and attitudes that define the church's cultural environment.

Some signals are intentional. Leaders celebrate faithfulness, reinforce discipleship, and organize ministry around the church's mission. Other signals may develop unintentionally through neglect, inconsistency, or the quiet tolerance of practices that do not align with the church's convictions. Whether intentional or not, these signals shape how members understand the life and purpose of the church.

Because culture forms through observable patterns, leadership must remain attentive to the signals being communicated within the congregation. What is celebrated encourages repetition. What is tolerated gradually becomes accepted. What is corrected reinforces the standards that guide the community. Even moments of crisis reveal the deeper patterns that have been forming within the church over time.

The chapters that follow examine several of these visible signals. Each illustrates how leadership actions and congregational responses contribute to the church's cultural environment. By understanding these signals, leaders can more faithfully reinforce the convictions, direction, and mission that define the congregation's life.

When these signals remain aligned with biblical teaching and the church's stated convictions, culture becomes stable, healthy, and unified. The congregation learns not only through instruction but also through the consistent patterns of life that shape the body's shared experience.

Chapter Seven Embodied Authority and Symbolic Leadership

Leadership in the church is not expressed through statements alone. Authority is also communicated through visible behavior, consistent conduct, and the example leaders set before the congregation. Members of the church observe how leaders live, respond to challenges, and interact with others. Through these observations, the congregation begins to understand what the church truly believes and values.

Because leadership is highly visible, leaders' actions carry symbolic meaning. Decisions, attitudes, and personal conduct serve as signals that shape how members interpret the church's priorities. Even small actions can communicate powerful messages about humility, integrity, faithfulness, and responsibility. Over time, these signals contribute to the formation of culture within the congregation.

Scripture repeatedly emphasizes that leadership within the church is meant to be demonstrated through example. Leaders are not called merely to give instruction but to embody the principles they teach. Their lives provide a model that others can observe and follow. When leadership consistently reflects the church's convictions, the congregation gains a clearer understanding of how to live them out in everyday life.

Symbolic leadership also reinforces unity within the body. When leaders visibly demonstrate a commitment to the church's mission, members are encouraged to participate in that same work. When leaders show humility, patience, and faithfulness, those qualities begin to shape the congregation's attitudes. Leadership example becomes a form of instruction that operates alongside teaching and preaching.

However, the symbolic influence of leadership can also work in the opposite direction. If leadership behavior contradicts the church's values and mission, confusion and instability begin to develop. Members may struggle to understand which messages truly represent the convictions of the church. Over time, this inconsistency weakens trust and disrupts cultural stability.

For this reason, leadership must recognize that authority is always embodied. The personal conduct of leaders communicates as much as their words. When leaders live in alignment with the convictions, direction, and mission of the church, their example strengthens the congregation's cultural environment and reinforces the unity of the body.

Clothing and the Communication of Office

Throughout Scripture, clothing often functions as a visible symbol of authority, responsibility, and spiritual role. While garments themselves do not create authority, they frequently communicate the office or responsibility a person has been entrusted to carry. In this way, clothing can serve as a symbolic reminder of the role a leader occupies within the community of faith.

In Exodus 28, God instructed Moses to create specific garments for the priests who would serve in the tabernacle. These garments were not designed merely for appearance but to reflect the sacred responsibility of the priestly office. The text describes garments made "for glory and for beauty," emphasizing that the clothing itself communicated the significance of the role. The priest's attire distinguished his role and reminded the people that the service being performed was part of the worship of God.

These garments also reinforced accountability. Those who wore them were publicly identified as those entrusted with spiritual duties. The visible nature of the clothing served as a reminder that the office carried responsibility before both God and the people.

Zechariah 3:3–5 provides another example of clothing used symbolically. In the vision, Joshua the high priest is described as standing before the Lord wearing filthy garments. These garments symbolized the condition of the people and the need for cleansing. God then commands that the filthy garments be removed and replaced with clean clothing. The new garments represented restoration and the renewal of the priestly office.

This passage demonstrates that clothing can communicate spiritual realities beyond appearance. The change of garments signified a transformation of standing before God and a restoration of the authority to serve.

In the life of the modern church, clothing does not carry the same covenantal significance as the priestly garments described in the Old Testament. However, the principle of visible signals still applies. The way leaders present themselves can convey seriousness, humility, reverence, or carelessness. These signals shape how members perceive the responsibilities of leadership roles.

Because leadership is visible, appearance can become one of many ways authority is symbolically communicated. While clothing alone does not define spiritual authority, it can reinforce the dignity and responsibility of the office when approached with wisdom and humility. Leaders should therefore recognize that even outward presentation can contribute to the signals that shape the church's cultural environment.

Casualization and Perceived Authority

The way leaders present themselves influences how their authority is perceived within the church. Over time, many institutions have experienced a gradual shift toward increasing informality in appearance, language, and conduct. While casual approaches may appear approachable or relatable, they can also affect how leadership responsibility is understood by those observing it.

Authority within the church is not derived from clothing or outward appearance. It is rooted in calling, character, and faithfulness to the work God has entrusted to leaders. However, visible presentation still communicates signals to the congregation. When leadership becomes overly casual in conduct or appearance, members may begin to perceive the responsibilities of leadership as less serious or less distinct from everyday participation.

Scripture emphasizes that leaders should conduct themselves in ways that demonstrate maturity and spiritual integrity. In 1 Timothy 4:12 (KJV), Paul instructs Timothy: "Let no man despise thy youth; but be thou an example of the believers, in word, in conversation, in charity, in spirit, in faith, in purity." Timothy's authority was not established through age or status but through the example of his life. His conduct was to demonstrate the seriousness of his calling.

Titus 2:7 (KJV) reinforces this same principle: "In all things shewing thyself a pattern of good works: in doctrine shewing uncorruptness, gravity, sincerity." The leadership example was meant to reflect gravity and sincerity. These qualities communicate that the work of the church is worthy of reverence and faithful stewardship.

Casualization can sometimes weaken these signals if it unintentionally communicates indifference toward the responsibilities of leadership. When leaders approach their roles with visible seriousness and care, the congregation more easily recognizes the importance of the work being performed. Members are reminded that ministry involves stewardship, accountability, and service before God.

This does not mean that leaders must adopt rigid or artificial forms of presentation. Authenticity and humility remain essential qualities in Christian leadership. However, leaders should remain aware that their conduct and appearance communicate signals that influence how authority is perceived within the congregation.

When leadership reflects dignity, sincerity, and faithfulness, it reinforces the seriousness of the church's mission. These signals help establish an environment where members recognize the responsibilities of leadership and respond with respect, trust, and shared commitment to the work of the church.

Platform Posture and Congregational Expectation

The posture of leadership during public ministry communicates powerful signals to the congregation. The way leaders stand, speak, and conduct themselves when addressing the church shapes how members perceive the importance of the moment. Platform posture becomes one of the visible ways authority, reverence, and seriousness are communicated within the life of the congregation.

In Nehemiah 8:4–8 (KJV), Ezra the scribe stood upon a wooden pulpit built for the purpose of reading the Law to the people. As he opened the book, the people stood in reverence. Ezra read the law of God clearly, and the Levites helped the people understand what was being read. The physical arrangement of the gathering, including the raised platform and the attentive posture of the people, reinforced the seriousness of the moment. The Word of God was being proclaimed publicly, and the visible structure of the gathering communicated its importance.

This passage illustrates how posture and setting can shape the expectations of a congregation. Ezra did not simply read quietly among the crowd. The raised platform allowed the people to see and hear clearly, emphasizing the authority of the Scripture being presented. The posture of both the leader and the people reflected reverence for the Word of God.

Within the modern church, similar principles still apply. The way leaders conduct themselves when preaching, teaching, or guiding worship influences how members approach those moments. When leadership demonstrates attentiveness, clarity, and reverence, the congregation often responds with similar attitudes. Platform posture helps establish the tone of the gathering.

Conversely, when the platform is approached casually or without a clear structure, the congregation may interpret the gathering as informal or unimportant. Over time, these signals shape the expectations that members bring to worship services and teaching environments. Posture communicates whether the moment is an ordinary conversation or a sacred instruction.

For this reason, leaders should recognize that the platform carries symbolic significance. It represents a place where the Word of God is proclaimed and where the congregation gathers for instruction, encouragement, and correction. The posture of those who stand there communicates how seriously that responsibility is taken.

When leaders approach the platform with humility, reverence, and attentiveness, they reinforce the expectation that the Word of God deserves careful attention. The congregation learns through these signals that worship and teaching are moments of spiritual significance, worthy of respect and thoughtful engagement.

The Removal of Distinction and Its Effects

Leadership within the church carries a responsibility that is both spiritual and visible. While all believers share equal standing before God through Christ, Scripture also recognizes that certain individuals are entrusted with particular responsibilities within the life of the church. These responsibilities create a distinction of role, not of personal worth, but of stewardship and accountability.

Hebrews 5:4 (KJV) emphasizes this principle when speaking of spiritual leadership: “And no man taketh this honour unto himself, but he that is called of God, as was Aaron.” The office of spiritual leadership is not assumed casually or claimed through personal ambition. It is a calling that carries responsibility before God and before the people being served. The recognition of this calling establishes a clear distinction between leadership responsibility and general participation within the body.

The apostle Paul describes this stewardship in 1 Corinthians 4:1 (KJV): “Let a man so account of us, as of the ministers of Christ, and stewards of the mysteries of God.” Leaders within the church are described as stewards entrusted with sacred responsibilities. Their role involves teaching, guarding doctrine, and caring for the spiritual well-being of the congregation.

When these distinctions are clearly understood, the congregation benefits from healthy structure and accountability. Members recognize that leadership carries responsibility for guidance, teaching, and oversight. Leaders themselves are reminded that their authority is not personal privilege but entrusted stewardship.

However, when the distinction between leadership responsibility and general participation blurs, confusion can arise. If leadership roles appear indistinguishable from ordinary participation, members may struggle to understand who is responsible for teaching, guidance, and decision-making within the church. Over time, this uncertainty can erode clarity and diminish leadership effectiveness.

Distinction does not require distance or superiority. Christian leadership is defined by humility and service rather than status. Yet the responsibilities entrusted to leaders must remain visible enough that the congregation understands the structure of spiritual care and accountability within the church.

For this reason, leadership should maintain clarity regarding roles and responsibilities within the body. When these distinctions remain healthy and properly understood, the church benefits from both unity and order. Members serve together as one body, while leadership faithfully fulfills the stewardship entrusted to it by God.

Servant Leadership Without Indistinguishability

Christian leadership is fundamentally defined by service. The authority entrusted to leaders in the church is not meant to elevate individuals above others but to guide, teach, and care for the people of God. Scripture consistently presents leadership as an act of stewardship and responsibility carried out for the benefit of the body.

Jesus provided the clearest example of this principle in John 13:3–5 (KJV). Knowing that the Father had given all things into His hands, Jesus took a towel and washed His disciples' feet. The act demonstrated that true authority in the kingdom of God is expressed through humble service. The one who possessed the greatest authority willingly performed a task associated with the lowest servant.

This example reshaped the understanding of leadership among Christ's followers. Authority was no longer measured by status or privilege but by willingness to serve others. Leaders were called to imitate the humility and care demonstrated by Christ Himself.

However, servant leadership does not eliminate the distinction of leadership responsibility. Hebrews 13:7 (KJV) instructs believers: "Remember them which have the rule over you, who have spoken unto you the word of God: whose faith follow, considering the end of their conversation." The passage acknowledges that certain individuals are entrusted with guiding and teaching the church. Their lives are meant to serve as examples that others can observe and follow.

These two truths exist together within the life of the church. Leaders are called to serve with humility, but they are also entrusted with real responsibility and authority. Servant leadership does not remove leadership; it defines the character with which leadership is exercised.

When the desire to emphasize humility leads to the removal of all visible leadership distinctions, confusion can result. Members may struggle to understand who is responsible for teaching, guiding, and protecting the church's doctrine. The intention to avoid hierarchy can unintentionally weaken the clarity needed for healthy leadership.

For this reason, the church must hold both principles together. Leadership must remain humble, service-oriented, and Christlike in character. At the same time, the responsibilities entrusted to leaders must remain visible so that the congregation understands who has been called to guide and care for the body.

When servant leadership is practiced without eliminating the distinction between responsibility and authority, the church benefits from both humility and clarity. Leaders serve faithfully, members follow with trust, and the body of Christ grows together in unity and maturity.

Chapter Eight
Worship Environment and Production Culture

The environment in which worship occurs communicates important signals about how a church understands the purpose of gathering. While the central focus of Christian worship is the glory of God and the proclamation of His Word, the physical setting, atmosphere, and structure of the service influence how members experience and interpret that purpose. The worship environment becomes one of the visible elements that contribute to the formation of church culture.

Throughout Scripture, worship gatherings carried an awareness of reverence and intentional structure. From the tabernacle and temple to the early gatherings of believers, worship was approached with a recognition that the people of God were assembling in response to His presence and authority. This awareness shaped both the conduct of the participants and the order of the gathering itself.

In many modern churches, technological capabilities have expanded the ways services are presented. Lighting, sound systems, stage design, projection screens, and digital media can assist communication and help large gatherings function effectively. These tools can support the church's mission when used wisely. They can make teaching more accessible, assist congregational singing, and help communicate information clearly.

However, technology can also shape the expectations members bring to worship. When the environment begins to resemble entertainment or performance, members may gradually interpret the gathering through the lens of production rather than participation. The congregation may shift from active worshippers to passive observers if the service's structure unintentionally communicates that the platform is the primary focus.

Production culture often emphasizes presentation quality, visual impact, and emotional atmosphere. While these elements are not inherently negative, they can reshape how members understand the purpose of worship if they become the dominant feature of the gathering. When production becomes central, the focus can subtly shift away from corporate worship of God toward the experience delivered to the audience.

Healthy churches recognize the difference between helpful tools and defining priorities. Technology and thoughtful presentation can support the clarity of teaching and the organization of worship, but they must remain servants of the church’s mission rather than replacements for it. The gathering of believers exists to glorify God, proclaim His Word, and encourage the body of Christ in faith and obedience.

For this reason, leaders must carefully consider the signals communicated through the worship environment. The platform's arrangement, the service's tone, and the balance between participation and presentation all contribute to how members interpret the purpose of worship. When the environment reinforces reverence, attentiveness to Scripture, and active participation, it strengthens a culture centered on worship and discipleship.

When these priorities remain clear, the church's environment supports the mission rather than overshadowing it. The gathering becomes a place where believers focus their attention on God, engage with His Word, and participate together in the life of the body of Christ.

Smoke, Lighting, and Symbolic Messaging

The visual environment of worship communicates powerful symbolic messages to a congregation. Elements such as lighting, atmosphere, stage design, and visual effects shape how people interpret the gathering's tone and purpose. Even when these elements are intended to support music or communication, they can influence how members perceive the meaning of worship.

Throughout Scripture, visible phenomena often accompanied moments when God revealed His presence. In Exodus 19:16–18 (KJV), when the Lord descended upon Mount Sinai, the scene was marked by thunder, lightning, thick cloud, and smoke. The mountain trembled, and the people were filled with awe. These signs did not exist to entertain or impress the people. They communicated the holiness, power, and majesty of God. The visible environment reinforced the seriousness of the moment and reminded the people that they were encountering the presence of the Lord.

This biblical example shows that visual elements can carry symbolic meaning. The sights and sounds surrounding the event communicated the character of God and the gravity of His covenant with His people. The environment helped shape the congregation's response, leading them toward reverence and humility.

The New Testament continues this emphasis on reverence in worship. Hebrews 12:28–29 (KJV) declares, "Let us have grace, whereby we may serve God acceptably with reverence and godly fear: For our God is a consuming fire." Worship is not merely a gathering of convenience or entertainment. It is the response of believers to God's holiness and authority.

In the modern church, lighting and atmospheric effects are often used to create visual emphasis or mood within worship services. These tools can help focus attention, assist communication, and support the flow of the gathering. However, they also communicate symbolic messages about what the church believes worship to be.

If visual effects dominate the environment, members may begin to associate worship with performance or emotional atmosphere rather than reverence before God. The congregation may focus on the service's sensory experience rather than its spiritual purpose of gathering. Over time, these signals can shape how people understand the nature of worship.

For this reason, leaders should remain thoughtful about the symbolic messages communicated through the worship environment. Visual elements should serve the purpose of worship rather than redefine it. When lighting, design, and atmosphere foster attentiveness to God and His Word, they can support the congregation's spiritual focus.

When these tools are used with wisdom and restraint, the worship environment helps direct attention to the holiness of God rather than to the production of the service. In this way, the visual setting supports a culture of reverence, humility, and genuine worship within the life of the church.

In consulting work, each church environment must be evaluated individually. Congregations differ in size, tradition, technology, and cultural context, and wise leadership requires careful analysis before offering recommendations. However, some practices communicate such strong symbolic messages that caution is appropriate.

In the case of stage smoke or theatrical atmospheric effects during a Sunday morning worship service, the symbolic signals often move the gathering toward performance rather than reverence. Because these effects are commonly associated with entertainment environments, their presence can unintentionally shape how members interpret the service's purpose.

For this reason, leaders should approach such elements with great caution. In most situations, restraint better protects the clarity and reverence of congregational worship.

Stage Design and Performance Posture

The physical arrangement of the worship platform communicates important signals about how a church understands the purpose of its gatherings. Stage design influences where attention is directed, how participants interact with the service, and whether the congregation perceives the gathering as an act of corporate worship or as a performance being presented to an audience.

In many churches, the platform serves a practical purpose. It allows the congregation to see and hear those leading worship, preaching the Word, and guiding the service. Clear visibility and sound are necessary for large gatherings, and thoughtful design can help the congregation remain engaged with what is being communicated. However, the stage's structure and emphasis can also shape the congregation's expectations.

When the platform becomes visually dominant or is designed primarily for presentation, the gathering's posture can gradually shift. The congregation may begin to view the service as something performed by those on the stage rather than something in which the entire body participates. This shift can change how members engage with worship, moving them from active participants to observers of what is taking place before them.

The apostle Paul addressed a similar concern regarding the focus of ministry in 1 Corinthians 2:1–5 (KJV). Paul explained that when he came to Corinth, he did not rely on "excellency of speech or of wisdom" but proclaimed the testimony of God with simplicity and dependence on the Spirit. He emphasized that his preaching was not intended to impress the listeners through persuasive presentation but to point them toward the power of God.

Paul's example highlights the importance of maintaining the proper focus in ministry. The goal of preaching and teaching is not to create admiration for the messenger but to direct attention toward the truth being proclaimed. The authority of the message comes from God rather than from the skill or presentation of the speaker.

Stage design and platform posture can either reinforce or weaken this principle. When the environment emphasizes the message and encourages congregational participation, the focus remains on worship and the proclamation of Scripture. When the environment emphasizes performance and presentation, attention can shift toward the individuals leading the service.

For this reason, leaders should remain aware that stage design communicates cultural signals. The arrangement of space, the prominence of certain elements, and the posture of those leading worship all influence how the congregation interprets the purpose of the gathering. When the platform supports humility, clarity, and attentiveness to God's Word, it reinforces a culture of worship centered on Christ rather than on presentation.

A healthy worship environment reminds the congregation that the gathering is not a performance to observe but a shared act of worship before God. The platform serves the mission of the church by supporting the clear proclamation of Scripture and encouraging the active participation of the body of Christ.

Darkened Rooms and Visual Focus

The physical environment of worship influences how the congregation directs its attention during a service. Lighting, visibility, and the arrangement of space all contribute to the atmosphere of the gathering and communicate subtle messages about where focus should be placed. One of the most common environmental decisions churches make concerns lighting in the sanctuary, particularly the practice of darkening the room while illuminating the platform.

Darkened rooms often create a strong visual contrast between the congregation and those leading the service. When the platform is brightly lit while the seating area remains dim, the visual center of the room naturally shifts toward the stage. This arrangement can increase visibility for speakers and musicians, but it can also shape how the congregation interprets the role of those leading the service.

Worship in Scripture consistently directs attention toward the holiness and majesty of God rather than toward the individuals leading the gathering. Psalm 96:9 (KJV) calls believers to "O worship the Lord in the beauty of holiness: fear before him, all the earth." The focus of worship is the Lord Himself. The gathered people of God come together to honor Him, hear His Word, and respond in reverence and obedience.

Lighting choices can either reinforce or redirect this focus. When the congregation remains visible to one another, the gathering retains a sense of corporate participation. Members are reminded that they are worshiping together as a body rather than watching a presentation. The shared visibility of the room communicates that the entire congregation is engaged in worship.

When the room is heavily darkened, however, the posture of the gathering can shift subtly. Individuals may feel less connected to the larger body and more oriented toward the illuminated platform. Over time, this arrangement can reinforce the perception that the service's primary activity occurs on the stage rather than among the congregation.

This does not mean that lighting adjustments are inherently inappropriate. Practical considerations, such as visibility, technology, and architectural limitations, often influence how churches manage lighting in their spaces. However, leaders should remain aware that lighting choices communicate symbolic signals about participation and focus.

When the environment supports corporate engagement and attentiveness to God, the congregation is reminded that worship is a shared act of reverence before the Lord. Thoughtful use of lighting can help maintain that focus by reinforcing the church's gathered nature rather than emphasizing the platform.

Volume, Emotion, and Sensory Stimulation

The sensory environment of worship also communicates important signals about the nature and purpose of the gathering. Sound levels, musical intensity, lighting effects, and emotional atmosphere all influence how members experience a service. While music and expression have long been part of worship, the balance between reverence and stimulation can shape how a congregation understands its time before God.

Music has always played a meaningful role in the lives of the people of God. Throughout Scripture, singing and instruments are used to praise the Lord, declare His works, and encourage the hearts of believers. When music supports congregational participation and directs attention to God, it strengthens the church's unity and spiritual focus.

However, the volume and emotional intensity of music can also affect the posture of worship. Extremely loud environments or highly stimulated atmospheres may shift the experience from reflection and reverence toward sensory immersion. When this occurs, the congregation may begin to interpret worship primarily through emotional response rather than through thoughtful engagement with God and His Word.

Ecclesiastes 5:1–2 (KJV) offers an important reminder regarding the attitude believers should bring when approaching God: "Keep thy foot when thou goest to the house of God, and be more ready to hear, than to give the sacrifice of fools… Be not rash with thy mouth, and let not thine heart be hasty to utter any thing before God." The passage calls for attentiveness, humility, and thoughtful reverence when entering the Lord's presence.

This principle suggests that worship should not only express joy and praise but also encourage reflection and attentiveness to God's voice. When the sensory environment becomes overwhelming, it can make quiet reflection and thoughtful listening more difficult for some members of the congregation.

Leaders must therefore consider how sound and atmosphere influence the posture of the gathering. Music that supports congregational singing, clear teaching, and moments of quiet reflection all contribute to a balanced environment of worship. These elements help maintain the focus on God rather than on the experience itself.

This does not mean that emotion has no place in worship. A genuine response to God often includes joy, gratitude, conviction, and reverence. However, emotional expression should naturally flow from the truth being proclaimed rather than be manufactured through sensory stimulation.

When the worship environment encourages both heartfelt praise and thoughtful reverence, the congregation can respond to God with sincerity and understanding. The sensory elements of the service then serve their proper role, supporting worship rather than redefining it.

Edification Versus Entertainment

The purpose of the gathered church is the spiritual edification of the body of Christ. While worship services may include music, teaching, prayer, and fellowship, these elements are intended to build up believers in faith, understanding, and obedience to God. The structure and content of the gathering should reinforce spiritual growth rather than provide an engaging experience.

Scripture repeatedly emphasizes that the assembly of believers exists to strengthen the church. In 1 Corinthians 14:26 (KJV), Paul explains the purpose of the gathering: "How is it then, brethren? when ye come together, every one of you hath a psalm, hath a doctrine, hath a tongue, hath a revelation, hath an interpretation. Let all things be done unto edifying." The central principle is that everything occurring within the assembly should contribute to the edification of the body.

This instruction reveals that the gathering is participatory and purposeful. Members bring their gifts, teaching, and encouragement to benefit others. The goal is mutual strengthening through the ministry of the Word, worship, and spiritual fellowship.

Colossians 3:16 (KJV) reinforces this emphasis on spiritual formation within worship: "Let the word of Christ dwell in you richly in all wisdom; teaching and admonishing one another in psalms and hymns and spiritual songs." Music within the church is not merely an emotional experience but a means of teaching and encouraging believers. The songs of the church communicate truth, reinforce doctrine, and remind the congregation of God's character and work.

When the purpose of worship remains centered on edification, the congregation learns, grows, and strengthens one another in faith. Members participate actively in the life of the church rather than observing it from a distance. Teaching, music, and prayer work together to deepen understanding and reinforce spiritual maturity.

However, when the structure of the gathering shifts toward entertainment, the focus can gradually change. Members may begin to evaluate services based on how engaging or enjoyable they are rather than on how they contribute to spiritual growth. The congregation may become consumers of a religious experience rather than participants in building one another up.

This shift does not usually occur intentionally. It often develops slowly as churches adopt practices that emphasize presentation, stimulation, or performance. Over time, these signals can reshape expectations about what worship is meant to accomplish.

For this reason, church leaders must continually return to the biblical purpose of the gathering. Every element of the service should contribute to the spiritual strengthening of the congregation. Music should teach truth, preaching should clearly proclaim the

Word of God, and the service's structure should encourage participation and attentiveness.

When the gathering remains centered on edification, the church grows in maturity and unity. The congregation leaves strengthened in faith, equipped for service, and reminded of the truth of God's Word. Worship then fulfills its proper role, building up the body of Christ rather than entertaining it.

Chapter Nine
Music as Theological Formation

Music has always played a central role in the worship life of God's people. From the psalms of Israel to the hymns of the early church, singing has been used to express praise, remember the works of God, and reinforce the truths of Scripture. Because songs are easily repeated and remembered, they often shape a congregation's beliefs and attitudes more deeply than many other forms of instruction.

The church does not sing merely to create atmosphere or emotional engagement. Music serves as a means of teaching and reinforcing theological truth. When believers sing together, they rehearse the doctrines of the faith, proclaim the character of God, and remind one another of the promises of Scripture. Through repetition, these truths become embedded in the congregation's memory.

Throughout history, the songs of the church have functioned as a form of discipleship. Hymns and spiritual songs have been used to teach the nature of God, the work of Christ, the hope of salvation, and the call to faithful living. Many believers can recall lines from songs long after sermons have faded from memory. In this way, music becomes a powerful instrument of theological formation within the life of the church.

Because music carries such influence, the content of what is sung deserves careful attention. The lyrics of worship songs communicate beliefs about God, salvation, the church, and the Christian life. If the words lack theological clarity, the congregation may gradually adopt incomplete or inconsistent ideas that are inconsistent with Scripture. Over time, repeated language shapes how believers understand their faith.

For this reason, leaders responsible for worship must approach music with discernment and responsibility. Song selection is not simply a matter of preference or musical style. It is a form of teaching that contributes to the spiritual formation of the congregation. The theology expressed in music should remain consistent with the doctrine the church proclaims in preaching and instruction.

Music also reinforces the congregation's shared identity. When believers sing the same truths together, they participate in a collective confession of faith. The act of singing unifies the church around the truths of the gospel and reminds members that they belong to a larger body of believers who share the same hope and commitment to Christ.

When music remains rooted in biblical truth and centered on the character and work of God, it strengthens the life of the church. The congregation learns through song, remembers through repetition, and participates together in declaring the truths of the Christian faith. In this way, music becomes not only an expression of worship but also an instrument through which the church's theology is continually formed and reinforced.

Lyrics as Doctrinal Instruction

The words sung in worship significantly influence a congregation's spiritual formation. Because songs are repeated frequently and remembered easily, the lyrics of worship music often become one of the most consistent sources of theological instruction within the life of the church. What believers sing week after week gradually shapes how they think about God, salvation, and the Christian life.

Colossians 3:16 (KJV) describes this role clearly: "Let the word of Christ dwell in you richly in all wisdom; teaching and admonishing one another in psalms and hymns and spiritual songs." In this passage, singing is not presented merely as expression or celebration. It is a means through which believers teach and encourage one another. The songs of the church communicate truth and reinforce the message of Scripture within the hearts of the congregation.

This instruction occurs through repetition. When a congregation sings the same truths regularly, those truths become familiar and deeply embedded in memory. Members carry these words with them throughout the week, recalling them in moments of prayer, reflection, and difficulty. In this way, the lyrics of worship songs function as a form of ongoing discipleship.

Because of this influence, the theological content of worship lyrics must be considered carefully. Songs communicate beliefs about the character of God, the work of Christ, the nature of salvation, and the response of believers. If the language used in worship lacks clarity or biblical grounding, the congregation may gradually absorb incomplete or imprecise ideas.

Historically, many of the great hymns of the church were written with strong doctrinal foundations. These songs explained the gospel, proclaimed the attributes of God, and reminded believers of the promises found in Scripture. Through singing, congregations learned theology in a memorable, communal way.

This principle remains important for the modern church. Leaders responsible for selecting music must recognize that every song chosen becomes part of the congregation's teaching ministry. The words sung on Sunday morning reinforce the beliefs the church seeks to cultivate among its members.

When lyrics faithfully reflect biblical truth, they strengthen the church's understanding of the gospel and reinforce the message proclaimed from the pulpit. Worship music then becomes more than musical expression. It becomes a shared declaration of faith that teaches, encourages, and reminds believers of the truth of God's Word.

Repetition and Emotional Reinforcement

Repetition is one of the most powerful tools in shaping memory and belief. In the life of the church, repeated phrases, melodies, and lyrical themes reinforce ideas that gradually become familiar and deeply embedded in the hearts of the congregation. Because music is both memorable and emotional, repetition within worship songs can strengthen the theological messages being communicated.

Scripture itself demonstrates the use of repetition in worship. Psalm 136 (KJV) repeatedly declares the phrase, "for his mercy endureth for ever," after each statement describing the works of God. The repeated line appears throughout the entire psalm, reinforcing the central truth that God's mercy remains constant and enduring. The repetition allows the congregation to participate in the declaration and ensures that the central message remains firmly fixed in the minds of those reciting it.

This pattern illustrates how repetition can function as a form of instruction. Each time the phrase is repeated, the listener is reminded again of the same theological truth. Over time, the repetition strengthens understanding and encourages reflection on the character of God.

Music within the church often follows a similar pattern. Choruses and refrains repeat key ideas, helping the congregation remember and internalize the song's message. When a repeated message reflects biblical truth, repetition can reinforce faith, foster gratitude, and strengthen the congregation's shared beliefs.

However, repetition can also intensify emotional response. Music naturally engages the emotions, and repeated phrases combined with musical progression can heighten the emotional atmosphere of a gathering. This can create powerful moments of collective expression as the congregation joins together in praise.

While emotion itself is not inappropriate in worship, leaders must remain attentive to the relationship between repetition and emotional reinforcement. If repetition emphasizes clear theological truth, it strengthens the congregation's understanding of God and His works. If repetition focuses primarily on emotional experience rather than strong doctrinal content, the song's emphasis may shift away from instruction and toward sensation.

For this reason, repetition in worship music should reinforce meaningful truth rather than extend the emotional moment. When repeated phrases proclaim the character of God, the work of Christ, and the hope of the gospel, they contribute to the spiritual formation of the congregation.

When used wisely, repetition allows believers to rehearse the truths of Scripture together. The congregation remembers the message, internalizes the meaning, and carries those words into daily life. In this way, repetition becomes a tool that strengthens both understanding and devotion within the life of the church.

Participation Versus Observation

Congregational singing has historically been one of the most participatory elements of Christian worship. When the church gathers, believers join together to praise God, confess the truth, and encourage one another through song. This shared expression reinforces the body's unity and reminds members that worship is a collective act rather than a presentation by a few individuals.

Ephesians 5:19 (KJV) describes this pattern clearly: "Speaking to yourselves in psalms and hymns and spiritual songs, singing and making melody in your heart to the Lord." The instruction assumes participation among believers. Members of the congregation are not merely listening to music; they are actively engaging with one another through the songs they sing. Worship becomes a shared declaration of faith within the community.

When congregational participation is emphasized, the entire body becomes involved in worship. Each member contributes by lifting their voice, reflecting on the words being sung, and joining with others in praise. This shared participation reinforces the idea that worship belongs to the whole church rather than to a particular group leading from the platform.

However, the structure of music within a service can influence whether members perceive themselves as participants or observers. When music is structured primarily as a performance, the congregation may gradually become passive listeners rather than active worshippers. Complex arrangements, unfamiliar melodies, or extended instrumental segments can unintentionally reduce the opportunity for congregational involvement.

Over time, this shift can change the posture of worship. Members may begin to experience the music portion of the service as something they watch rather than something they contribute to. The platform becomes the center of activity while the congregation becomes an audience.

The biblical pattern suggests a different emphasis. Songs within the church are intended to encourage shared expression and mutual edification. When believers sing together, they proclaim truth not only to God but also to one another. The congregation hears the voices of fellow believers declaring the same faith, reinforcing unity and shared conviction.

For this reason, leaders should consider how the structure of worship music encourages participation. Songs with accessible, clear lyrics and arrangements that support congregational singing help maintain the participatory nature of worship. When the congregation engages fully, the gathering reflects the biblical picture of believers encouraging one another through psalms, hymns, and spiritual songs.

When participation remains central, the church experiences worship as a shared act of devotion rather than as an event presented from the platform. The voices of the congregation become part of the testimony of faith, declaring together the truth and greatness of God.

Industry Influence and Congregational Formation

The music used in worship services is not developed in isolation. Many churches draw songs from a broader Christian music industry that produces albums, concerts, and worship resources for congregations around the world. These resources can be helpful, providing churches with new music that proclaims the gospel and encourages believers in their faith. However, the broader industry also shapes how worship music is written, presented, and distributed.

The structure of the music industry often emphasizes production quality, wide appeal, and emotional engagement. Songs are frequently developed for large gatherings, recordings, or broadcast environments. As a result, the musical style and lyrical approach of these songs may reflect the priorities of large audiences and commercial distribution rather than the specific needs of a local congregation.

When churches adopt music primarily from external sources without careful evaluation, the theological and cultural influences of those sources can gradually shape the congregation's identity. The language used in songs, the themes emphasized in lyrics, and the style of musical presentation may begin to define the expectations members bring to worship. Over time, the congregation's understanding of worship can be influenced by the patterns established within the industry itself.

Romans 12:2 (KJV) offers a guiding principle for evaluating these influences: "And be not conformed to this world: but be ye transformed by the renewing of your mind." The passage encourages believers to examine the influences shaping their thinking and to ensure that their lives are formed by the truth of God rather than by the patterns of the surrounding culture.

This principle applies to worship as well. Churches must evaluate whether the music they adopt reflects biblical priorities and supports the congregation's mission. Songs should communicate clear theological truth, encourage congregational participation, and direct attention toward God rather than toward performance or emotional experience alone.

The goal is not to reject all music produced outside the local church. Many songs written and shared across the broader Christian community have strengthened believers for generations. Instead, leaders must exercise discernment, selecting music that aligns with the congregation's doctrine, mission, and cultural health.

When church leaders carefully evaluate the influences shaping their worship music, they protect the theological formation of the congregation. The songs chosen for worship then reinforce the truth of Scripture and support the spiritual growth of the church rather than unintentionally introducing ideas or patterns that weaken its focus.

Sound, Reverence, and Sacred Posture

The sound environment of a worship service influences the posture with which a congregation approaches God. Music, volume, rhythm, and tone all shape how people experience the gathering and how they direct their attention during worship. Because these elements affect both the emotional and physical atmosphere of the service, they contribute to the cultural signals communicated within the church.

Psalm 95:6 (KJV) calls believers to a posture of reverence before God: "O come, let us worship and bow down: let us kneel before the Lord our maker." The verse emphasizes humility and recognition of God's authority. Worship is not merely an expression of enthusiasm but a response to the holiness and sovereignty of the Lord.

Music can help encourage this posture when it directs attention toward the character and works of God. When songs emphasize gratitude, praise, and the truth of Scripture, the congregation is reminded of why they have gathered and whom they are worshiping. The sound of the congregation singing together reinforces the shared acknowledgment that God alone is worthy of worship.

However, the volume and intensity of sound can also influence how worship is experienced. Extremely loud environments or overwhelming musical intensity may create excitement, but they can also reduce opportunities for reflection and attentiveness. When individuals cannot clearly hear the words being sung or the voices of fellow believers, the sense of shared participation may weaken.

Reverence in worship does not require quietness alone. Scripture includes examples of joyful praise and celebration among the people of God. Yet even within joyful expression, the focus remains on honoring the Lord rather than on the sensory experience itself.

Leaders should therefore consider how the sound environment contributes to the posture of the congregation. When sound and music reinforce reverence, the gathering becomes an opportunity for believers to respond together in worship. The congregation recognizes the presence of the Lord, acknowledges His authority, and collectively honors Him with sincere praise.

Chapter Ten
Reverence and the Casualization of Sacred Space

The physical space where a church gathers conveys important signals about how the congregation understands worship. Buildings, seating arrangements, décor, and the room's overall atmosphere shape how people approach the gathering. While the presence of God is not confined to any building, the environment in which believers assemble can influence the posture with which they enter into worship.

Throughout Scripture, places associated with the worship of God were approached with reverence. Whether in the tabernacle, the temple, or gatherings among the early believers, the people of God recognized that their assembly was not ordinary. They were gathering to hear the Word of God, to pray, and to respond together to His authority. This awareness shaped how they conducted themselves when they came together.

In many modern contexts, however, cultural patterns of informality have gradually influenced the atmosphere of church gatherings. As society has moved toward greater casualness in everyday life, the same tendencies often appear within worship environments. The result can be a space that feels indistinguishable from other public gatherings, such as lectures, performances, or community events.

Casual environments are not inherently wrong. Simplicity, accessibility, and hospitality can help people feel welcome within a church community. However, when the physical environment communicates little distinction between ordinary activities and sacred gathering, the sense of reverence that Scripture encourages may weaken.

Sacred space does not require elaborate architecture or expensive decoration. The early church often met in homes and simple places of assembly. What distinguished these gatherings was the understanding that the people were meeting before God. The atmosphere of the gathering reflected attentiveness, humility, and seriousness in worshiping the Lord.

The casualization of sacred space can occur gradually. When visual cues, physical arrangements, and behavioral expectations mirror those of entertainment venues or casual public spaces, members may begin to approach the gathering with the same posture they bring to other social events. Over time, this can reshape how worship is understood and experienced.

For this reason, church leaders should remain attentive to the signals the environment sends to the congregation. The goal is not to create unnecessary formality or distance but to preserve an atmosphere that reflects the significance of worship. When the environment encourages attentiveness to God and respect for the gathering, it reinforces the reverent posture Scripture calls believers to maintain.

A healthy worship environment reminds the congregation that the gathering is not merely another event in the weekly schedule. It is a moment when the people of God assemble to hear His Word, honor His name, and strengthen one another in faith. When reverence remains present within the space of worship, the church is continually reminded of the holiness and authority of the God they serve.

Coffee in Worship Settings

The atmosphere of a worship gathering communicates how the church understands the purpose of its assembly. Small practices within the service environment can shape the posture with which members approach worship. Even ordinary activities, such as eating or drinking, can influence whether the gathering is perceived as a sacred assembly or a casual social event.

In many modern churches, beverages such as coffee are commonly present during worship services. For some congregations, this practice is intended to foster a welcoming, relaxed environment. Hospitality is an important aspect of Christian fellowship, and churches often desire to remove unnecessary barriers that might prevent people from feeling comfortable within the gathering.

However, the presence of food or drink within the worship environment can also communicate subtle signals about the nature of the gathering. When the church assembly begins to resemble a casual meeting or social setting, the distinction between worship and ordinary activity may become less clear. Members may begin to approach the service with the same posture they bring to everyday gatherings rather than with the attentiveness Scripture encourages.

The apostle Paul addressed a related concern in 1 Corinthians 11:20–22 (KJV). In Corinth, believers were approaching the Lord's Supper in a manner that reflected casual eating rather than reverent participation in a sacred remembrance. Paul corrected this behavior, reminding the church that the gathering was not simply another meal. The assembly required order, respect, and recognition of the spiritual significance of what was taking place.

The principle behind Paul's instruction highlights the importance of distinguishing between ordinary activities and sacred gatherings. The church assembly exists for worship, teaching, prayer, and the strengthening of the body of Christ. When common daily activities become central to the service, they can unintentionally blur that distinction.

This does not mean that fellowship and hospitality should be removed from church life. Shared meals, coffee, and conversation can be meaningful expressions of community when they occur before or after the worship gathering. These moments strengthen relationships and provide opportunities for encouragement among believers.

However, leaders should carefully consider how practices in the worship setting shape the congregation's posture. When the environment encourages attentiveness, reverence, and participation, the gathering more clearly reflects its purpose as an assembly before God.

By maintaining a thoughtful distinction between fellowship activities and the act of worship itself, the church preserves the sense that the gathering is a moment set apart. The congregation comes together not merely to socialize but to hear the Word of God, honor His name, and respond together in faith and obedience.

Behavior at the Altar

Throughout Scripture, the altar represents a place of encounter between God and His people. It is associated with sacrifice, repentance, prayer, and surrender before the Lord. Because of this significance, the behavior of those approaching the altar has historically reflected reverence and humility.

In Exodus 3:5 (KJV), when Moses encountered the presence of God at the burning bush, the Lord instructed him, “Draw not nigh hither: put off thy shoes from off thy feet, for the place whereon thou standest is holy ground.” The command did not change the physical nature of the ground itself, but it recognized that God's presence made the moment sacred. Moses was called to approach with humility and awareness of God's holiness.

This passage illustrates a broader principle regarding sacred encounters. When individuals come before God in prayer, confession, or surrender, the posture of the moment should reflect the seriousness of that encounter. The altar has traditionally served as a visible place where believers respond to the conviction of the Holy Spirit, seek forgiveness, or dedicate themselves anew to God's work.

Behavior at the altar communicates cultural signals to the congregation. When the altar is approached with reverence, humility, and attentiveness to God, the church recognizes the spiritual importance of the moment. Members observe that prayer and repentance are meaningful acts of faith, worthy of careful attention.

However, when the altar area is treated as an ordinary space of conversation or casual activity, the symbolic meaning of the moment can weaken. If individuals move through the area without recognizing its purpose, the congregation may gradually lose the sense that the altar is a place of response before God.

The altar itself does not possess supernatural power, nor is it required for prayer or repentance. Believers may call upon the Lord anywhere. Yet the visible place of response within a church gathering carries symbolic value. It provides a space where members publicly express their need for God's help, forgiveness, and guidance.

For this reason, leaders should encourage behavior around the altar that reflects reverence and attentiveness. When the congregation observes that the altar is treated with respect, it reinforces the understanding that moments of prayer and surrender are significant within the life of the church.

When approached with humility and seriousness, the altar becomes a place where believers encounter the grace of God, seek His direction, and respond to the work of the Holy Spirit within their lives.

Alcohol at Christian Events

The presence of alcohol at Christian gatherings has long been a subject of discussion among believers. Scripture does not present a single universal rule governing every social setting, yet it consistently calls believers to exercise wisdom, self-control, and consideration for others' spiritual well-being. Within the context of church events and ministry environments, the presence of alcohol can communicate signals that influence the culture of the congregation.

Romans 14:21 (KJV) provides an important principle regarding the conduct of believers: "It is good neither to eat flesh, nor to drink wine, nor any thing whereby thy brother stumbleth, or is offended, or is made weak." The apostle Paul emphasizes that personal freedom should never be exercised in a way that harms another believer's spiritual conscience. The well-being of the body of Christ takes priority over individual preference.

A similar concern appears in 1 Corinthians 8, where Paul addresses the issue of food sacrificed to idols. Some believers understood that eating such food carried no spiritual meaning, while others associated it with past practices of idolatry. Paul's instruction focused not on asserting personal liberty but on protecting the conscience of fellow believers. He warned that exercising freedom without regard for others could unintentionally lead someone into spiritual confusion or distress.

These passages establish a broader principle for Christian conduct within communal settings. Actions that may be personally permissible can still affect the community's spiritual environment.

In church gatherings, leaders must consider how practices shape the congregation's culture and witness.

Alcohol, in particular, can communicate mixed messages within ministry environments. For some individuals, it may represent an ordinary social practice. For others, it may be associated with past struggles, addiction, or moral concern. When alcohol becomes present at church-related events, members may interpret its presence in different ways, creating potential tension within the community.

Because church gatherings exist to encourage spiritual growth and unity, leaders must carefully evaluate how such practices affect the congregation. The goal of ministry environments is to strengthen believers, protect the vulnerable, and maintain a clear witness to the surrounding community.

This does not mean that the same policy must govern every situation. Churches differ in tradition, cultural context, and conviction. However, the guiding principle remains consistent. Decisions within ministry environments should prioritize the spiritual well-being of the congregation and the unity of the body of Christ.

When leaders approach these matters with humility and careful discernment, they help maintain a culture that values both freedom and responsibility. The church becomes a place where believers consider one another with love, choosing actions that strengthen faith and preserve unity within the community.

Although this author strongly recommends refraining from alcohol in church settings, it must also be recognized that some church-related gatherings take place in public settings, such as parks or restaurants, where the environment cannot be fully controlled. In such settings, not every individual present may share the same commitment to honoring God. Because of this reality, leaders must remain aware that secular practices can gradually enter ministry environments when clear boundaries are not maintained.

Phones, Selfies, and Digital Distraction

Modern technology has introduced new forms of communication and connection that influence nearly every area of daily life. Mobile phones, social media platforms, and digital communication tools allow individuals to remain constantly connected to information and to one another. While these technologies offer many practical benefits, they also pose challenges when introduced into environments intended for worship and reflection.

The presence of mobile devices during church gatherings can gradually reshape how individuals engage with the service. Phones provide immediate access to messages, notifications, and online content that compete for attention. Even brief interruptions can divert attention from the message being preached, the prayers being offered, or the songs being sung. Over time, this pattern can reduce the attentiveness with which members approach the gathering.

The practice of taking photos or recording personal content during worship services introduces an additional layer of distraction. When individuals focus on capturing moments for social media or personal documentation, their attention may shift from participating in worship to curating a digital experience. This shift can subtly change the posture of the gathering from reflection and reverence toward observation and documentation.

Psalm 46:10 (KJV) offers a principle that speaks to the posture of worship: "Be still, and know that I am God." The verse calls believers to pause amid the noise and activity of life to recognize the Lord's presence and authority. Stillness allows the mind and heart to focus on God without the constant interruptions that often characterize daily life.

The church gathering provides an opportunity for this kind of attentiveness. When believers set aside distractions and focus on worshiping God, they create space for reflection, instruction, and spiritual renewal. The absence of constant digital interruption allows the congregation to listen carefully to Scripture, respond in prayer, and engage fully in the life of the body.

This does not mean that technology has no place within the church. Mobile devices can provide access to digital Bibles, sermon notes, and other helpful resources. However, the presence of these tools should not undermine the attentiveness and reverence appropriate to the gathering.

For this reason, leaders should encourage practices that minimize unnecessary distraction during worship. When members approach the service with a posture of attentiveness and stillness, the congregation is better able to hear the Word of God and respond together in faith.

By maintaining an environment where digital distractions are limited, the church protects the focus of the gathering. The congregation is reminded that worship is not another moment for constant communication or documentation but an opportunity to pause, listen, and respond to the voice of God.

The Gradual Diminishing of Sacred Distinction

Throughout the life of the church, the distinction between sacred activity and ordinary life has served as an important reminder of the holiness of God and the purpose of worship. While believers live their daily lives in the world, Scripture consistently calls the people of God to maintain a clear awareness that certain moments, practices, and gatherings are set apart for the worship and service of the Lord.

Sacred distinction does not mean that buildings, objects, or locations possess spiritual power on their own. Rather, the distinction arises from the purpose for which believers gather and the posture with which they approach that gathering. When the church gathers to hear the Word of God, to pray, and to worship together, the moment is set apart by the people's intention and reverence.

However, cultural patterns often move toward gradual informality. Practices that once reflected reverence and distinction may slowly give way to casual habits that mirror the broader culture. When this occurs gradually, the change may go largely unnoticed. Each small adjustment may appear harmless in isolation, yet the cumulative effect can reshape how the congregation perceives the significance of worship.

The apostle Paul addresses the importance of maintaining distinction in 2 Corinthians 6:17 (KJV), where believers are instructed, "Wherefore come out from among them, and be ye separate, saith the Lord." The call to separation does not mean isolation from society but rather the preservation of a life shaped by the values and holiness of God rather than by the patterns of the surrounding culture.

Within the life of the church, this principle applies to the signals communicated by behavior, environment, and practice. When the church intentionally maintains practices that reflect reverence and attentiveness to God, it reinforces the understanding that the gathering of believers is not merely another social event. It is a moment set apart for worship, instruction, and spiritual formation.

The diminishing of sacred distinction often occurs slowly rather than through deliberate change. Over time, small shifts in behavior, environment, and expectations can accumulate until the difference between worship gatherings and ordinary events becomes less clear. When this distinction fades, the posture members adopt toward the gathering may change as well.

For this reason, leaders must remain attentive to the cultural signals communicated within the church. Maintaining a healthy sense of sacred distinction helps preserve reverence, clarity of purpose, and attentiveness to God. The goal is not to create unnecessary rigidity but to ensure that the gathering of believers continues to reflect the holiness and authority of the One they worship.

When the church maintains this awareness, the congregation is reminded that worship is a response to the living God. The gathering becomes a moment where believers set aside ordinary distractions and approach the Lord with humility, gratitude, and reverence.

Chapter Eleven
Speech Culture and Edification

The words spoken within a church community contribute significantly to the culture that develops among its members. Speech reflects the values, attitudes, and priorities that shape the life of the congregation. Over time, the patterns of communication that become normal within the church influence how members interact with one another and how they understand their responsibilities within the body of Christ.

Scripture consistently emphasizes the importance of speech among believers. Words have the power to encourage, correct, instruct, and strengthen others in their faith. When church communication reflects truth, kindness, and humility, it fosters an environment where spiritual growth and unity can flourish.

The culture of speech within a congregation is often shaped by the example set by leadership. Pastors, elders, and ministry leaders influence how members communicate by the tone, clarity, and care with which they speak. When leaders demonstrate patience, respect, and thoughtful instruction, these patterns often reflect in the broader church community.

Conversely, patterns of speech that include criticism, careless language, or unnecessary conflict can weaken the sense of unity within the body. When negative communication becomes common, members may begin to feel discouraged, defensive, or hesitant to participate fully in the life of the church. Over time, these patterns can erode trust and reduce the effectiveness of ministry efforts.

The church gathering also provides opportunities for speech that strengthen believers' faith. Teaching, testimony, prayer, and encouragement all involve spoken communication that reinforces the truth of Scripture and the shared mission of the church. Through these interactions, members learn from one another and grow together in understanding and maturity.

Because speech carries such influence, believers are called to approach their words with care. Communication within the church should reflect the character of Christ and the purpose of the gathering. Words should strengthen rather than weaken, clarify rather than confuse, and encourage rather than divide.

When speech within the congregation consistently reflects truth and grace, the church's culture becomes one of mutual encouragement and spiritual growth. Members are reminded that their words are not merely casual conversation but part of the shared responsibility of building up the body of Christ.

Biblical Standards for Speech

Scripture provides clear guidance on how believers should speak to one another. Because words have the power to influence attitudes, relationships, and spiritual growth, the Bible consistently calls Christians to use speech that strengthens rather than harms the community of faith. The language used within the church should reflect the character of Christ and edify the body.

Ephesians 4:29 (KJV) provides one of the most direct instructions concerning speech: “Let no corrupt communication proceed out of your mouth, but that which is good to the use of edifying, that it may minister grace unto the hearers.” The apostle Paul emphasizes that speech among believers should build others up rather than tear them down. Words should foster spiritual growth and encourage, strengthening the faith of those who hear them.

This instruction highlights the responsibility believers carry in everyday conversation. Communication within the church includes teaching, discussion, correction, and encouragement, yet each of these should be expressed in ways that reflect grace and care for others. The goal of speech is not merely the exchange of information but the strengthening of the community of faith.

Colossians 4:6 (KJV) reinforces this principle: "Let your speech be alway with grace, seasoned with salt, that ye may know how ye ought to answer every man." Speech that is gracious and thoughtful reflects wisdom and self-control. Such communication demonstrates respect for others while still conveying truth with clarity.

The metaphor of speech being "seasoned with salt" suggests both preservation and careful preparation. Words should be chosen thoughtfully so that they communicate truth effectively while maintaining a tone that reflects humility and care for those listening.

Within the life of the church, these standards shape the overall culture of communication. When members speak with grace and intentionality, the congregation develops an environment where people feel encouraged and supported in their spiritual growth. Teaching becomes clearer, correction becomes constructive, and relationships remain strengthened rather than strained.

For this reason, leaders should model these biblical standards in their own communication. When pastors and ministry leaders consistently speak with grace and clarity, they set an example that influences the broader culture of the congregation. Members learn not only through instruction but also through the patterns of speech they observe.

When the church consistently follows these biblical standards, communication becomes a tool for edification rather than conflict. The words spoken within the congregation reflect the character of Christ and strengthen the body of believers.

Coarse Language in Informal Settings

The culture of speech within a church is not formed only during formal gatherings. Conversations in hallways, small groups, ministry meetings, and informal interactions also shape the overall tone of communication within the congregation. These everyday moments often reveal the speech patterns that members consider acceptable within the community.

Scripture addresses the importance of maintaining purity and wisdom in language, even in ordinary conversation. Ephesians 5:4 (KJV) instructs believers: "Neither filthiness, nor foolish talking, nor jesting, which are not convenient: but rather giving of thanks." The passage reminds believers that certain forms of speech do not reflect the character of those who belong to Christ. Instead of language that degrades or distracts from godly living, believers are called to cultivate speech marked by gratitude and respect.

This instruction applies not only to public teaching but also to private and informal conversation. When coarse language becomes common in casual settings, it can gradually shape the broader community's tone. What begins as humor or informal expression may slowly reshape expectations about what kind of speech is appropriate within the church.

James 3:9–12 (KJV) further emphasizes the responsibility believers carry in their use of words. James observes that the tongue can both bless God and speak harmfully toward others. He compares this contradiction to a fountain that produces both fresh and bitter water. The point is clear: speech that honors God should remain consistent across every setting of life.

Within the church community, informal settings often shape communication culture as much as formal teaching does. Members observe how leaders and fellow believers speak during ordinary moments. If language remains respectful and thoughtful in these settings, it reinforces the standards presented in Scripture.

However, when coarse or careless speech becomes common in informal environments, the distinction between Christian conversation and everyday cultural language may begin to fade. Over time, this can weaken the sense that church speech should reflect the character of Christ.

For this reason, believers are called to maintain consistency in their words regardless of the setting. Conversations that occur before or after services, during ministry activities, or in casual fellowship should reflect the same care for speech that Scripture encourages in teaching and worship.

When the church maintains this consistency, the culture of communication strengthens the congregation's unity and spiritual health. Words become instruments of encouragement, gratitude, and truth, helping to build an environment where believers grow together in faith and maturity.

Humor, Sarcasm, and Cultural Tone

Humor can play a positive role within the life of a church community. Laughter often strengthens relationships, eases tension, and helps people feel connected. In healthy settings, appropriate humor can create warmth and encourage fellowship among believers. However, the type of humor that becomes common within a congregation also contributes to the cultural tone that develops among its members.

Because humor often carries subtle messages, it can influence how people speak to one another and how seriously certain matters are treated. Jokes, sarcasm, and playful remarks may appear harmless in the moment, yet they can shape expectations about communication and behavior within the community. Over time, recurring patterns of humor shape the atmosphere of conversation within the church.

Scripture warns about the potential harm that careless humor can create. Proverbs 26:18–19 (KJV) states: "As a mad man who casteth firebrands, arrows, and death, so is the man that deceiveth his neighbour, and saith, Am not I in sport?" The passage illustrates how harmful words can be excused as humor even when they cause damage. A person may claim that a statement was only a joke, yet the words themselves still carry consequences.

Sarcasm in particular can blur the line between humor and criticism. While it may be intended as playful or witty, sarcasm often communicates indirect disapproval or mockery. When this form of speech becomes common within a community, it can gradually shape a culture where subtle criticism is normalized through humor.

Within the church, the tone of communication should reflect the character of Christ. Humor that encourages joy, gratitude, and fellowship can strengthen relationships among believers. At the same time, humor that humiliates, criticizes, or trivializes serious matters can weaken trust and diminish mutual respect within the body.

Leaders play an important role in establishing the tone of humor within the congregation. When pastors and ministry leaders model thoughtful, respectful speech, members often follow suit. The communication patterns leadership demonstrates often become the patterns adopted by the broader community.

For this reason, believers should approach humor with discernment. Laughter and joy have an appropriate place in Christian fellowship, yet the tone of humor should remain consistent with the church's values. Words spoken in jest should not undermine the dignity, unity, or encouragement that the body of Christ is called to maintain.

When humor reflects kindness and wisdom, it contributes positively to the church's culture. The congregation experiences both joy and mutual respect, strengthening relationships while maintaining a tone that honors God and builds up the community of faith.

Gossip Disguised as Prayer

Communication within the church is meant to strengthen unity and encourage spiritual growth. Yet one of the more subtle ways unhealthy speech can appear within a congregation is when gossip is presented in a form that appears spiritually acceptable. In some situations, personal information about others may be shared under the guise of prayer requests or spiritual concern, even though the manner of sharing spreads unnecessary or harmful details.

The intention behind prayer is to bring needs before God and to encourage believers to support one another in times of difficulty. When handled with care and discretion, prayer requests allow the church to bear one another's burdens and demonstrate compassion. However, when private matters are discussed broadly without wisdom, the line between prayer and gossip can become blurred.

Scripture warns about the divisive nature of gossip. Proverbs 16:28 (KJV) states, "A froward man soweth strife: and a whisperer separateth chief friends." Gossip can damage relationships, create suspicion, and weaken trust within a community. Information shared without care can spread quickly, often reaching individuals who have no responsibility or ability to help address the situation.

When gossip is disguised as spiritual concern, it can be even harder to recognize. Language that appears caring or prayerful may still convey details that harm another person's reputation or privacy. Over time, this practice can create an environment where members feel hesitant to share personal struggles, fearing that their situation may become widely discussed.

Healthy communication within the church requires discernment regarding what information should be shared and with whom. Not every difficulty needs to be discussed publicly, and many situations are best handled privately by those directly responsible for providing care and guidance. Prayer for others can occur without revealing unnecessary personal details.

Leaders play an important role in shaping this culture. When pastors and ministry leaders demonstrate discretion and respect for personal matters, they set a standard that influences the broader congregation. Members learn that protecting the dignity and privacy of others is an important aspect of Christian love.

When prayer is practiced with wisdom and integrity, it strengthens the unity of the church. Believers support one another without spreading unnecessary information, and the community becomes a place where individuals feel safe seeking help and encouragement. In this way, communication remains focused on edification rather than division, preserving the trust essential to healthy church life.

Language as Cultural Formation

The language used within a church community plays a significant role in shaping the congregation's culture. Words are not merely tools for communication. They reveal attitudes, reinforce values, and influence how members understand the life of the church. Over time, the patterns of speech that become normal within a congregation help shape the community's tone and character.

Jesus emphasized the importance of speech when He said in Matthew 12:36 (KJV), "But I say unto you, That every idle word that men shall speak, they shall give account thereof in the day of judgment." This statement reminds believers that words carry weight and responsibility. Speech is not insignificant in the eyes of God, and the language people use reflects the condition of the heart.

Because language carries such influence, repeated patterns of speech gradually form expectations within the church. Words of encouragement strengthen faith and unity. Thoughtful correction promotes growth and accountability. Clear teaching reinforces truth and helps believers understand the Word of God. These patterns foster a culture in which communication supports the spiritual development of the congregation.

At the same time, careless language can shape a church's culture in less constructive ways. Persistent criticism, sarcasm, gossip, or harsh speech may gradually create a tense, distrustful atmosphere. Even when such language appears harmless in isolated moments, repeated patterns can influence how members treat one another and how they approach ministry together.

For this reason, the language leaders carry particular influence. Pastors, teachers, and ministry leaders often set the tone for communication within the congregation. When leadership consistently models gracious, truthful, and respectful speech, members are more likely to adopt similar patterns in their own interactions.

The culture of language within a church is therefore formed over time through daily conversation, teaching, and shared interaction. Members observe how others speak, what topics are emphasized, and how disagreements are handled. These observations gradually shape expectations for how communication should occur within the community.

When language reflects humility, encouragement, and biblical truth, the church becomes a place where words strengthen rather than weaken relationships. Communication contributes to the unity and spiritual maturity of the body. In this way, language becomes an instrument through which the church's culture is continually formed and reinforced.

Chapter Twelve Hospitality, Community, and Inclusion

Hospitality has long been recognized as an important expression of Christian life. Throughout Scripture, believers are encouraged to welcome others, demonstrate kindness, and create environments where people can experience the care and fellowship of the body of Christ. When practiced faithfully, hospitality strengthens relationships within the church and reflects the love that Christ has shown to His people.

The church gathering is often the primary place where hospitality is experienced. New visitors, long-time members, and individuals exploring faith all encounter the congregation's culture through how they are received and included. Small gestures, such as greetings, conversation, and a willingness to assist others, can communicate warmth and openness, helping people feel connected to the community.

Community within the church grows when members actively engage with one another beyond the formal structure of the service. Conversations before and after gatherings, shared meals, participation in ministry, and prayer support all contribute to the development of meaningful relationships. These interactions strengthen the sense that the church is not merely an event but a living body of believers who care for one another.

Inclusion within the church also reflects the gospel itself. The message of Christ invites people from every background to respond to the grace of God. As a result, the church becomes a place where individuals who may differ in age, experience, or personal history can gather together in shared faith and purpose. This unity demonstrates the transforming power of the gospel within the life of the community.

However, hospitality and inclusion require thoughtful attention. Churches must ensure that welcoming practices do not become superficial gestures that fail to develop meaningful connections. True hospitality extends beyond greeting someone at the door. It involves ongoing care, an interest in others' lives, and a willingness to integrate new people into the church's relationships and activities.

Leaders play a central role in establishing this environment. When pastors and ministry leaders model attentiveness to visitors and demonstrate genuine care for members, the congregation often follows that example. Over time, these patterns become embedded in the church's culture.

Healthy hospitality balances openness with purpose. While the church should welcome people from all backgrounds, the gathering remains centered on worship, teaching, and spiritual formation. Inclusion does not remove the church’s commitment to truth but invites individuals to encounter that truth within a community marked by kindness and care.

When hospitality, community, and inclusion are practiced with sincerity, the church becomes a place where people experience both welcome and spiritual growth. Members support one another, visitors feel valued, and the congregation reflects the unity and compassion that characterize the body of Christ.

The Handshake Culture

The way members greet one another during a church gathering communicates important signals about the congregation's culture. Simple acts such as handshakes, greetings, and brief conversations can convey warmth, openness, and mutual respect.

These small gestures often form the first impression that visitors and new members receive when they enter the church community.

Romans 15:7 (KJV) encourages believers with this instruction: "Wherefore receive ye one another, as Christ also received us to the glory of God." The command reminds the church that welcoming others reflects the grace that believers themselves have received through Christ. When members greet one another with kindness and sincerity, they express Christian fellowship.

Handshake culture, or the practice of intentionally greeting others during church gatherings, can help reinforce this atmosphere of welcome. When members acknowledge one another with a handshake, a smile, or a brief conversation, the congregation becomes more than a group of individuals attending the same event. It begins to function as a community where people recognize and care for one another.

For visitors, these interactions can be especially meaningful. A warm greeting may reduce the sense of uncertainty that often accompanies attending a new church. Simple acts of kindness communicate that the congregation values the presence of those who have come to worship alongside them.

At the same time, hospitality must remain thoughtful and respectful. Not every individual is comfortable with physical contact or extended attention, particularly if they are new to the environment. Leaders and members alike should approach greetings with sensitivity, allowing warmth without creating pressure or discomfort.

Handshake culture works best when it arises naturally from genuine concern for others rather than from rigid expectations. When members sincerely acknowledge one another, these moments reinforce the sense that the church is a body of believers joined together in fellowship.

Over time, these patterns of greeting contribute to the broader culture of the church. Members become accustomed to recognizing one another, offering encouragement, and welcoming newcomers. Through these simple interactions, the congregation reflects the hospitality and acceptance that Scripture calls believers to practice.

When greetings are sincere and consistent, the church gathering becomes a place where people feel recognized and valued. The practice of welcoming one another then becomes a small but meaningful expression of the unity and love that characterize the body of Christ.

Welcoming the Stranger

The presence of visitors within a church gathering provides an opportunity for believers to demonstrate hospitality and care. Individuals who attend a church for the first time often arrive with uncertainty about what to expect. The way members respond to newcomers communicates important signals about the congregation's character and priorities.

Hebrews 13:2 (KJV) encourages believers with this instruction: “Be not forgetful to entertain strangers: for thereby some have entertained angels unawares.” The passage reminds the church that hospitality toward the unfamiliar is not a mere courtesy but an expression of obedience to God. Welcoming the stranger reflects humility and awareness that every person entering the gathering carries value and dignity before the Lord.

For many visitors, the first moments within a church environment shape their understanding of the community. Being greeted warmly, offered assistance in finding seating or resources, and invited into conversation can help remove the sense of isolation that newcomers sometimes feel. These gestures communicate that the church is attentive to those who enter its doors.

Welcoming the stranger also requires intentional awareness. Established members of a congregation often arrive with existing relationships and routines that naturally draw them toward familiar conversations. Without careful attention, visitors may unintentionally remain unnoticed while members interact primarily with those they already know.

When the congregation develops a culture of attentiveness to newcomers, this pattern begins to change. Members look for individuals who appear unfamiliar, introduce themselves, and offer simple assistance. These actions help visitors feel acknowledged and respected as they participate in the gathering.

At the same time, hospitality should remain genuine rather than forced. Visitors are often sensitive to whether greetings arise from sincere care or from obligation. Authentic kindness, simple conversation, and a willingness to listen often communicate welcome more effectively than formal gestures alone.

Leaders can help shape this culture by modeling attentiveness to new attendees and encouraging members to do the same. Over time, the congregation begins to view hospitality not as a program but as a natural expression of Christian fellowship.

When a church consistently welcomes the stranger with humility and kindness, it reflects the character of the gospel itself. The congregation becomes a place where individuals are received with respect and care, providing an environment where visitors can encounter both the truth of God's Word and the love of His people.

Insider Circles and Closed Groups

Healthy church communities naturally form friendships and close relationships over time. Shared experiences in ministry, long-term fellowship, and personal connection often lead members to develop strong bonds with one another. These relationships can strengthen the life of the congregation by providing encouragement, accountability, and mutual support.

However, when these relationships become closed circles that are difficult for others to enter, they can unintentionally create barriers within the church community. New members and visitors may find it challenging to connect if the congregation's social structure revolves around established groups that rarely expand to include others.

Scripture warns against attitudes that create divisions within the community of faith. James 2:1–4 (KJV) addresses the problem of showing partiality within the assembly. In the passage, individuals are treated differently based on appearance and status, resulting in unequal treatment among believers. James identifies this behavior as inconsistent with the faith that believers profess.

While modern church situations may not mirror the exact circumstances described in the passage, the principle remains relevant. Favoritism, exclusion, or unintentional social barriers can weaken the unity that the church is called to maintain. When certain groups become perceived as insiders while others remain on the outside, the sense of shared belonging within the body of Christ can diminish.

Insider circles often develop without deliberate intention. Long-standing friendships, shared ministry involvement, or common backgrounds naturally draw people together. Yet when these circles remain closed, they can make it difficult for new members to develop meaningful connections within the congregation.

Church leaders and members alike share responsibility for maintaining an environment where relationships remain open and welcoming. Simple practices such as inviting new individuals into conversations, including others in fellowship activities, and introducing members across different groups can help create a more inclusive community.

When members intentionally remain attentive to those who may feel disconnected, the congregation reflects the unity that Scripture encourages. Relationships continue to grow, but they remain open rather than exclusive. New members can find their place within the community, strengthening the sense that the church functions as one body rather than a collection of separate groups.

By maintaining awareness of how relationships shape the church's social environment, congregations can preserve a culture of hospitality and unity. The church becomes a place where long-standing friendships coexist with openness toward new connections, reflecting the shared identity believers have in Christ.

Staff Post-Service Behavior

The behavior of church leaders immediately following a service communicates important signals to the congregation. While the sermon, worship, and ministry elements of the gathering are central, the actions of pastors, staff, and ministry leaders after the service often shape how members and visitors interpret the church's culture.

Acts 6:1–4 (KJV) describes a moment in the early church when practical needs began to affect the unity of the congregation. The apostles responded by establishing a structure that allowed both spiritual leadership and practical service to function properly. The passage highlights the importance of leadership attention and responsibility within the life of the church.

In the context of a modern congregation, the immediate aftermath of a service offers leaders an opportunity to engage with the people they serve. Members may wish to ask questions, share concerns, or express encouragement. Visitors may be seeking a personal connection with leadership before deciding whether to return.

When church staff quickly retreat to private areas or remain inaccessible after the service, the congregation may interpret this behavior as a sign of distance or disinterest. Even when such actions are unintentional or driven by scheduling demands, they can create the perception that leadership is removed from the people.

Conversely, when leaders remain present and available after the service, the church's culture communicates openness and accessibility. Simple interactions such as greeting members, speaking with visitors, or offering prayer reinforce the relational nature of pastoral leadership.

These moments also allow leaders to observe the congregation in ways that formal meetings or structured programs cannot. Conversations after the service often reveal concerns, encouragement, or emerging needs within the church community. Remaining present provides valuable insight into the congregation's life.

This does not suggest that leaders must remain indefinitely after every gathering. Practical responsibilities and personal boundaries are necessary. However, intentional presence after the service signals that leadership values personal connection and remains attentive to the church's needs.

Over time, these patterns shape expectations within the congregation. When leaders consistently demonstrate availability and attentiveness, the church's culture reflects relational leadership rather than organizational distance. Members and visitors alike recognize that the church's leadership remains engaged with the people they serve.

Partiality and Biblical Community

The health of a church community depends on how its members understand their shared identity in Christ. Scripture teaches that believers come from many different backgrounds, cultures, and life circumstances, yet their faith and participation unite them in the body of Christ. This unity forms the foundation for a genuine Christian community.

Galatians 3:28 (KJV) expresses this truth clearly: "There is neither Jew nor Greek, there is neither bond nor free, there is neither male nor female: for ye are all one in Christ Jesus." Paul's words emphasize that the distinctions that often divide people in society do not define the standing of believers within the church. In Christ, every believer shares the same spiritual identity and value.

This biblical teaching challenges the church to resist forms of partiality that can quietly emerge within community life. Preferences based on social status, financial position, family background, or personal familiarity can gradually influence how people are received and included within the congregation. When such distinctions shape relationships, the unity described in Scripture begins to weaken.

Partiality can appear in subtle ways. Certain individuals may receive greater attention because of influence, long-standing relationships, or visible roles within the church. Others may find themselves less noticed or less included in the life of the congregation. Even when unintentional, these patterns communicate unequal value within the community.

Biblical community requires a different posture. The church is called to recognize each believer as a fellow member of the body of Christ. Every person who enters the gathering stands before God with equal spiritual worth, and the community of faith should reflect that reality in its relationships and interactions.

When members consciously reject partiality, the church's culture begins to reflect the unity Scripture describes. Conversations become more inclusive, fellowship expands beyond familiar circles, and the congregation grows stronger through the participation of many different individuals.

Leaders also play an important role in reinforcing this principle. By modeling impartiality in their interactions and encouraging a spirit of inclusion within the congregation, they help cultivate a community that reflects the unity of believers in Christ.

A church that practices biblical community becomes a place where individuals are received not according to status or familiarity but according to their shared identity in Christ. Such a culture strengthens fellowship, deepens unity, and allows the congregation to function more faithfully as the body of Christ.

PART IV
The Corruption of Culture Through Neglected Governance

Culture rarely collapses suddenly. In most churches, cultural decline occurs slowly as leadership neglects the structures that once safeguarded the congregation's convictions. When governance weakens, behavior gradually drifts away from the values and mission that originally defined the church.

The earlier sections of this work explained how culture is formed through conviction, leadership example, and the visible signals present in church life. Culture grows where beliefs, practices, and expectations consistently reinforce one another. When these elements remain aligned, the church develops stability and unity.

However, culture can also deteriorate when leadership fails to guard that alignment. When standards are no longer enforced, correction becomes rare, or leadership hesitates to address unhealthy behavior, the church's environment begins to shift. Practices that once would have been corrected may slowly come to be tolerated. Over time, tolerance becomes normalization.

Neglected governance does not simply create organizational problems. It produces spiritual consequences. When leaders fail to guide, correct, and protect the life of the congregation, the church's cultural environment becomes vulnerable to confusion and disorder. Members may struggle to understand what the church truly believes or expects.

Scripture repeatedly warns spiritual leaders about their stewardship responsibilities within the community of faith. Leadership involves more than teaching and encouragement. It also includes protecting the church's health by maintaining order, addressing error, and preserving unity.

This section examines how cultural corruption often begins with small moments of neglected leadership. When governance weakens, predictable patterns begin to emerge. Authority becomes unclear, accountability fades, and the shared life of the congregation gradually shifts away from its original convictions.

Understanding these patterns helps leaders recognize early signs of cultural drift before it causes greater damage. Healthy governance does not suppress spiritual life. It protects the conditions in which spiritual life can flourish.

The chapters that follow explore how neglected governance contributes to cultural decline and how churches can guard against these patterns through faithful leadership and clear accountability.

Chapter Thirteen
The Slow Erosion of Conviction

Cultural decline within the church rarely begins with open rejection of biblical truth. More often, it begins with small compromises that appear harmless at the time. Convictions that were once clearly understood gradually lose their clarity as practices change and leadership hesitates to address emerging inconsistencies.

Conviction functions as the foundation of church culture. Values express what leadership truly believes, and those beliefs shape the direction of the church's vision and mission. When convictions remain strong and clearly reinforced, the life of the congregation tends to remain stable. Members understand the principles that guide the church and the boundaries that protect its purpose.

However, when convictions are no longer reinforced through teaching, leadership, and governance, they begin to weaken. Practices may slowly shift to accommodate convenience, cultural pressure, or personal preference. Over time, behaviors that once would have raised concern may become normal within the congregation.

This erosion often occurs gradually enough that it is difficult to detect in its early stages. Each change may appear small or insignificant when viewed in isolation. Yet the cumulative effect of many small compromises can alter the character of the church in significant ways.

Leaders play a critical role in preserving the congregation's conviction. When leadership consistently teaches and models the church's beliefs, members are reminded of the principles that guide their shared life. Clear leadership helps ensure that conviction remains visible and active within the community.

Conversely, when leadership hesitates to address areas of drift, the congregation may interpret silence as approval. Behaviors that conflict with the church's stated values may continue without correction, allowing new patterns to take root within the culture.

Over time, these patterns influence how members understand the church's identity. Convictions that were once clearly defined may become less visible in daily practice. New members may enter the congregation without fully understanding the beliefs that once shaped its culture.

For this reason, maintaining conviction requires ongoing attention. Leaders must remain willing to teach clearly, address inconsistencies when they arise, and reinforce the principles that define the church's mission. When conviction is actively maintained, the church retains the cultural stability necessary to carry out its calling faithfully.

When Correction Ceases

Correction plays a necessary role in the health of any community that seeks to follow biblical instruction. Within the church, correction is not intended as punishment or personal criticism. Rather, it functions as a protective measure that helps preserve unity, accountability, and spiritual maturity within the body of believers.

Proverbs 29:1 (KJV) warns of the consequences that arise when correction is repeatedly resisted: "He, that being often reproved hardeneth his neck, shall suddenly be destroyed, and that without remedy." The proverb highlights the danger of rejecting correction. When individuals continually refuse guidance, the consequences of that resistance eventually become severe.

The principle also applies to the life of the church. When leadership no longer practices correction, unhealthy behaviors may continue without challenge. Practices that conflict with the church's convictions may persist simply because no one is willing to address them. Over time, the absence of correction allows patterns to develop that reshape the congregation's culture.

Correction serves an important clarifying function. When leaders address behavior that contradicts the church's values and mission, they reinforce the standards that guide the community. Members gain a clearer understanding of what the church believes and what is expected within the life of the congregation.

However, when correction ceases, that clarity begins to fade. Individuals may assume that certain behaviors are acceptable simply because they remain unchallenged. The silence of leadership can unintentionally convey approval, even when it was never intended.

This absence of correction often produces confusion within the church. Members may struggle to understand where the boundaries of conduct exist, and the distinction between conviction and preference may become unclear. Without consistent guidance, cultural expectations begin to shift.

Healthy correction requires wisdom, humility, and patience. Scripture consistently presents correction as an act of care rather than condemnation. When carried out with a spirit of restoration, it helps believers grow in maturity and strengthens the unity of the church.

For this reason, leaders must remain willing to address issues that threaten the congregation's health. Correction preserves clarity, protects conviction, and helps maintain the cultural integrity of the church. When practiced faithfully, it reinforces the standards that guide the community and supports the spiritual growth of those within it.

When Preference Overrides Principle

The health of a church culture depends on whether decisions are guided by biblical conviction or by personal preference. While preferences naturally exist within any congregation, they must never replace the principles that define the church's mission and identity. When preference begins to override principle, the church's direction slowly shifts away from its original convictions.

Galatians 1:10 (KJV) addresses the tension between pleasing people and remaining faithful to God: "For do I now persuade men, or God? or do I seek to please men? for if I yet pleased men, I should not be the servant of Christ." In this passage, Paul emphasizes that the servant of Christ cannot allow the approval of others to become the controlling motivation for leadership decisions.

Within church life, preference can influence many areas, including ministry style, worship practices, organizational priorities, and leadership decisions. While some preferences may be harmless, problems arise when they begin to shape the church's direction more strongly than its stated convictions.

When leaders consistently adjust decisions to satisfy competing preferences, the clarity of the church's mission begins to weaken. Members may receive mixed signals about what truly matters. Over time, the congregation may begin to interpret leadership decisions as attempts to maintain comfort rather than to pursue biblical purpose.

This shift often occurs gradually. A small adjustment may be made to accommodate a group's preferences, followed by another change intended to avoid conflict. Individually, each decision may appear reasonable. Collectively, however, these changes can begin to reshape the church's culture.

Principle provides stability amid these pressures. When leadership decisions remain anchored to clearly stated convictions, the church retains its direction even when disagreement arises. Members may not always share the same preferences, but they can understand the principles guiding the decisions.

Leaders, therefore, carry the responsibility of distinguishing between preference and principle. Preferences may be considered with wisdom and care, but they must never displace the biblical convictions that define the church's identity and mission.

When the principle remains the governing authority, the church preserves clarity in both leadership and culture. Decisions consistently reflect the convictions of the congregation rather than the shifting preferences of individuals, allowing the church to pursue its mission with confidence and unity.

When Growth Increases Complexity

Growth within the church is often viewed as a sign of health and spiritual vitality. As new individuals join the congregation and ministries expand, the opportunities for discipleship and service increase. However, growth also introduces new layers of complexity that must be addressed through thoughtful leadership and clear governance.

Acts 6:1 (KJV) records a moment in the early church when expansion created new challenges: "And in those days, when the number of the disciples was multiplied, there arose a murmuring of the Grecians against the Hebrews, because their widows were neglected in the daily ministration." The rapid growth of the early Christian community produced practical difficulties that required careful attention from leadership.

The problem described in this passage did not arise from rebellion or doctrinal error. Instead, it emerged from the increased complexity of serving a larger and more diverse congregation. As the number of believers grew, the systems that had once functioned effectively began to strain under the demands of the expanding ministry.

This pattern often appears in modern churches as well. Structures that worked well for a smaller congregation may become insufficient as attendance increases and ministries multiply. Communication becomes more difficult, responsibilities expand, and coordination between leaders becomes more necessary.

Without intentional organization, growth can produce confusion rather than unity. Ministries may begin to overlap, responsibilities may become unclear, and members may feel overlooked within the larger community. These challenges do not necessarily indicate spiritual weakness, but they do reveal the need for appropriate structure.

The early church's response demonstrates the importance of adapting governance to the realities of growth. Leaders recognized the emerging problem and added additional structure to ensure the congregation's needs were met. By establishing clear roles and responsibilities, they preserved both unity and effectiveness within the growing community.

Healthy leadership recognizes that growth requires thoughtful stewardship. As the church expands, governance structures must develop alongside it. Clear organization allows ministries to function smoothly and helps ensure that members continue to receive care and attention.

When leaders respond wisely to the complexity created by growth, the church remains stable and unified. Rather than allowing expansion to produce disorder, the congregation gains new capacity to serve its members and pursue its mission with clarity and purpose.

When New Leaders Lack Foundational Memory

Leadership transition is a natural part of the life of any church. Over time, new leaders emerge, new staff members are appointed, and younger generations begin to assume responsibility within the congregation. These transitions can bring energy, new ideas, and renewed enthusiasm for ministry. At the same time, they can create challenges when the church's historical convictions are not clearly remembered or preserved.

Judges 2:10 (KJV) describes a similar moment in the history of Israel: "And also all that generation were gathered unto their fathers: and there arose another generation after them, which knew not the Lord, nor yet the works which he had done for Israel." The passage reflects the danger that arises when the memory of foundational truths and experiences is not effectively passed from one generation to the next.

Within the church, foundational memory refers to the shared understanding of why certain convictions, structures, and practices were established. These decisions often emerged from careful reflection, previous challenges, and the accumulated wisdom of earlier leaders. When those reasons are forgotten, the practices themselves may appear unnecessary or outdated to newer leaders.

Without this historical understanding, leadership decisions may begin to change established patterns without recognizing the purpose those patterns once served. Structures that protected the mission of the church may be removed, not because they were harmful, but because their original intent is no longer understood.

This situation does not usually arise from deliberate disregard for the church's convictions. More often, it results from the incomplete transmission of institutional knowledge. When leadership transitions occur without intentional teaching about the church's history and guiding principles, the connection between past convictions and present decisions can weaken.

Healthy governance recognizes the importance of preserving this foundational memory. Written values, vision statements, mission statements, and policies serve as tools for communicating the church's identity across generations of leadership. These documents provide continuity even as individuals change.

Leaders also play an important role in teaching the history and convictions of the church to those who follow them. Mentorship, clear communication, and intentional documentation help ensure that new leaders understand the principles that shaped the church's culture.

When foundational memory is preserved, leadership transitions strengthen the church rather than destabilize it. New leaders bring fresh perspectives while remaining anchored to the convictions that define the congregation. In this way, the church maintains continuity of purpose while continuing to grow and develop across generations.

Institutional Stability Without Spiritual Depth

A church may appear stable on the surface while still experiencing spiritual weakness beneath the surface. Structures may function properly, ministries may continue operating, and attendance may remain steady. Yet these outward signs of stability do not always indicate genuine spiritual vitality within the congregation.

Revelation 3:1 (KJV) records Christ's message to the church in Sardis: "I know thy works, that thou hast a name that thou livest, and art dead." The warning reveals that a church may possess a reputation for life while lacking true spiritual strength. External appearance and internal condition do not always match.

Institutional stability often develops when systems, leadership structures, and routines continue to operate smoothly over time. Committees meet regularly, ministries follow established schedules, and administrative processes function without disruption. From an organizational standpoint, the church may appear healthy and well-managed.

However, structure alone cannot sustain spiritual life. When the church's practices become primarily procedural rather than devotional, the congregation may gradually lose its sense of spiritual urgency. Activities continue, but the deeper purpose behind those activities begins to weaken.

This condition sometimes arises when governance becomes disconnected from spiritual leadership. Policies and structures may remain in place, but the spiritual convictions that originally motivated those systems may fade from daily practice. The organization continues to function, yet the community's spiritual depth continues to diminish.

Scripture consistently calls the church to maintain both order and spiritual vitality. Structure can protect the church's mission, but it cannot replace the work of the Holy Spirit or the faithful devotion of believers. Institutional strength must remain connected to genuine spiritual life.

Leaders are responsible for guarding both aspects of church health. Governance should preserve order and clarity, while teaching, prayer, and spiritual discipline sustain the life of the congregation. When these elements remain connected, the church maintains both structural stability and spiritual depth.

The warning given to the church in Sardis reminds leaders that outward success should never replace spiritual examination. A congregation may appear strong in reputation while quietly weakening in devotion. Faithful leadership continually calls the church back to genuine spiritual life so that its outward stability reflects an authentic and living faith.

Chapter Fourteen
The Withdrawal of Moral Courage

Leadership within the church requires more than organizational ability or public communication. It also requires moral courage. Moral courage is the willingness to uphold biblical conviction even when doing so may produce discomfort, disagreement, or resistance. Without this courage, leadership gradually becomes hesitant to address issues that affect the health of the church.

Moral courage becomes necessary whenever conviction and pressure collide. At times, leaders must make unpopular decisions, correct harmful behavior, or maintain standards that conflict with cultural expectations. These moments test whether leadership will remain anchored to biblical principles or adjust direction to avoid conflict.

When moral courage is present, leadership provides clarity and stability for the congregation. Members understand that decisions are guided by conviction rather than by shifting pressures. Even when individuals disagree with certain decisions, they can recognize that those decisions are rooted in clearly stated principles.

However, as moral courage wanes, leadership may become reluctant to confront difficult situations. Problems that require attention may be postponed or quietly ignored. Conversations that should occur may be avoided to maintain temporary peace within the congregation.

This hesitation can have significant cultural consequences. When issues remain unaddressed, members may begin to interpret silence as acceptance. Behaviors that once conflicted with the church's convictions may persist without correction, gradually reshaping the community's expectations.

Over time, the absence of moral courage weakens leadership authority. Members may become uncertain about what the church truly believes or what standards remain in place. Without clear leadership, the church's cultural direction may begin to drift.

Scripture repeatedly calls spiritual leaders to exercise courage in protecting the life of the congregation. Leadership involves both encouragement and correction, both compassion and conviction. Faithful leadership requires the willingness to act when action is necessary, even when doing so may be difficult.

When moral courage remains active within leadership, the church retains clarity in both belief and practice. Leaders demonstrate that conviction is not merely spoken but lived. In this way, the congregation is guided with integrity, and the church's cultural stability is preserved.

Fear of Offense

One of the most common pressures facing church leadership is the fear of offending others. Leaders often desire to maintain harmony within the congregation and avoid unnecessary conflict. While peace within the church is valuable, the desire to avoid offense can sometimes influence decisions in ways that weaken conviction.

John 12:43 (KJV) describes individuals who struggled with this tension: "For they loved the praise of men more than the praise of God." The passage reveals the danger of prioritizing human approval over faithfulness to God. When the desire for acceptance outweighs the responsibility to uphold truth, leadership becomes compromised.

Within the life of the church, fear of offense may appear in subtle ways. Leaders may hesitate to address behaviors that conflict with biblical teaching because they fear upsetting certain individuals or groups. Sermons may avoid difficult passages of Scripture, and conversations that require correction may be postponed indefinitely.

While the intention behind this hesitation is often to preserve unity, the long-term effect can be the opposite. When important issues remain unaddressed, confusion grows within the congregation. Members may begin to wonder whether the church truly believes the convictions it once proclaimed.

Avoiding offense also places leadership in a difficult position. When decisions are guided primarily by others' reactions, the direction of the church becomes unstable. Different groups within the congregation may hold competing expectations, and leadership may feel pressure to satisfy each one.

Scripture consistently teaches that faithfulness to God must remain the primary concern of spiritual leadership. Leaders are called to teach truth with humility and love, but they cannot allow the fear of human approval to determine their message or decisions.

This does not mean that leaders should be careless in communicating the truth. Biblical leadership combines courage with compassion. Difficult matters should be addressed with patience, clarity, and respect for those involved.

When leaders overcome the fear of offense, they provide stability for the church. The congregation understands that decisions are guided by conviction rather than by shifting public expectations for approval. This clarity strengthens both the authority of leadership and the cultural health of the church.

Softened Doctrine

Doctrine forms the theological foundation of the church. Through the teaching of Scripture, believers come to understand the character of God, the nature of salvation, and the responsibilities of Christian life. When doctrine is clearly taught and faithfully upheld, the congregation gains stability in belief and direction.

2 Timothy 4:3–4 (KJV) warns of a time when doctrinal clarity would be resisted: "For the time will come when they will not endure sound doctrine; but after their own lusts shall they heap to themselves teachers, having itching ears; And they shall turn away their ears from the truth, and shall be turned unto fables." Paul describes a situation in which individuals prefer teaching that affirms their desires rather than instruction that challenges them with truth.

Softened doctrine often develops gradually rather than through open rejection of biblical teaching. Leaders may begin to emphasize certain aspects of Scripture while avoiding passages that address more difficult topics. Over time, the congregation may hear frequent messages of encouragement and comfort while receiving less instruction in repentance, discipline, and obedience.

While encouragement is an essential part of Christian teaching, a consistent avoidance of difficult truths weakens the doctrinal foundation of the church. Members may develop an incomplete understanding of the Christian life if teaching focuses only on themes that are easily accepted.

This pattern can also affect how the church approaches moral and theological questions. When doctrine is softened to avoid controversy, the congregation may become uncertain about what the church actually believes. Important issues may remain undefined or ambiguous to maintain broad agreement.

Scripture presents a different model for church leadership. Faithful teaching includes the whole counsel of God, including passages that challenge, correct, and call believers toward greater faithfulness. Sound doctrine guides both belief and behavior.

Leaders are responsible for maintaining doctrinal clarity within the congregation. Teaching should remain grounded in Scripture and should address both encouraging and corrective aspects of biblical instruction.

When doctrine remains clear and faithfully taught, the church retains a strong theological foundation. Members are equipped to understand their faith more deeply and to live in accordance with the truths revealed in Scripture. This clarity strengthens both the congregation's spiritual life and the church's cultural stability.

Silence on Holiness

Holiness has always been central to the identity of God's people. Scripture consistently calls believers to live lives that reflect the character and nature of God. Holiness is not merely an abstract theological idea; it is the practical expression of devotion to God in daily conduct.

1 Peter 1:15–16 (KJV) presents this call clearly: "But as he which hath called you is holy, so be ye holy in all manner of conversation; Because it is written, Be ye holy; for I am holy." The passage reminds believers that the call to holiness flows directly from the nature of God Himself. The life of the believer is intended to reflect the character of the One who has called them.

Within the church, teaching on holiness guides how believers live, speak, and conduct themselves in the world. It clarifies the distinction between the values of the kingdom of God and the patterns of the surrounding culture. Through this teaching, the church understands that faith involves both transformation and belief.

However, in some congregations, the topic of holiness gradually becomes less visible in public teaching. Sermons may focus primarily on encouragement, personal fulfillment, or practical advice while giving less attention to the call for personal sanctification. Over time, members may hear little instruction about the spiritual discipline and moral responsibility that accompany the Christian life.

This silence can have cultural consequences within the church. Without regular teaching on holiness, the boundaries between Christian living and broader cultural behavior may become less clear. Members may increasingly rely on personal judgment rather than on biblical guidance when making moral decisions.

The absence of teaching does not diminish the importance of holiness, but it can reduce the congregation's awareness of it. When the call to holiness is rarely addressed, believers may assume it is less essential to the life of faith than Scripture presents it.

Faithful leadership seeks to maintain balance in biblical instruction. Teaching on grace, encouragement, and forgiveness remains vital, yet these themes must exist alongside the consistent call to holiness. The Christian life includes both the assurance of salvation and the responsibility to pursue godly character.

When the church continues to teach holiness with clarity and humility, the congregation gains a deeper understanding of what it means to follow Christ. Members are reminded that faith shapes both belief and behavior. This instruction helps preserve the distinct identity of the church as a community called to reflect the character of God.

Avoidance of Discipline

Discipline within the church is often one of the most difficult responsibilities of spiritual leadership. Because it involves confronting sin and addressing harmful behavior, leaders may feel strong pressure to avoid it altogether. Yet Scripture consistently teaches that discipline is necessary for maintaining the spiritual health of the church.

1 Corinthians 5 records a situation in which serious moral sin had been tolerated within the Corinthian church. Rather than addressing the issue, the congregation had allowed the situation to continue. Paul rebuked the church for its inaction and instructed them to take corrective measures to protect the community's integrity.

The passage demonstrates that discipline is not motivated by hostility or personal judgment. Its purpose is the restoration of the individual involved and the protection of the congregation. When sin is openly tolerated, it shapes the church's culture and weakens the community's moral clarity.

Paul illustrated this danger by comparing tolerated sin to leaven spreading through dough. A small amount, when left unchecked, eventually affects the whole. In the same way, unaddressed wrongdoing can gradually reshape the expectations of behavior within the church.

Avoidance of discipline often begins with understandable hesitation. Leaders may fear conflict, public criticism, or the potential loss of members. Because discipline can be uncomfortable and emotionally difficult, there is a strong temptation to delay or ignore situations that require correction.

However, when discipline is consistently avoided, the long-term consequences can be significant. Members may become uncertain about what standards the church actually upholds. Individuals who are struggling with sin may receive no guidance or accountability, and the congregation may gradually lose confidence in the leadership's willingness to protect the church's integrity.

Scripture presents discipline as a form of loving correction intended to restore rather than to condemn. When carried out with humility and care, it helps individuals recognize the seriousness of sin and encourages repentance and reconciliation.

Faithful leadership must therefore balance compassion with responsibility. Ignoring sin does not protect the church; it allows harmful patterns to continue unchecked. By addressing issues when they arise, leaders demonstrate their commitment to the spiritual well-being of both individuals and the congregation.

When discipline is practiced with wisdom and grace, it strengthens the church's culture. Members understand that the community takes holiness seriously while still offering restoration to those who seek repentance. This balance helps preserve both the integrity and the unity of the body of Christ.

Cultural Accommodation

The church exists within the broader context of its culture, yet Scripture repeatedly calls believers to live according to God's standards rather than the patterns of the world. Maintaining this distinction is essential to preserving the church's spiritual identity and witness.

Romans 12:2 (KJV) provides this instruction: “And be not conformed to this world: but be ye transformed by the renewing of your mind, that ye may prove what is that good, and acceptable, and perfect, will of God.” The verse highlights the contrast between conformity to worldly patterns and transformation through a renewed mind shaped by God’s truth.

Cultural accommodation occurs when the church gradually adopts the attitudes, practices, or priorities of the surrounding culture in ways that weaken biblical conviction. This shift often begins with the intention of becoming more relatable or accessible to those outside the church. While thoughtful engagement with society can support the church's mission, unexamined accommodation can slowly erode the distinctiveness of the Christian life.

In some cases, cultural accommodation manifests itself through the adoption of values that conflict with biblical teaching. In other situations, it emerges through changes in language, priorities, or practices that place greater emphasis on cultural approval than on spiritual conviction. Over time, these adjustments can reshape the congregation's expectations.

This process rarely occurs through sudden or deliberate rejection of Scripture. Instead, it often develops gradually as leaders and members attempt to respond to cultural pressures. Small compromises made for the sake of acceptance or relevance may accumulate until the church begins to reflect the culture around it more than its convictions.

Scripture consistently calls believers to a different pattern of life. Transformation begins with the renewal of the mind through God's Word. As the church remains rooted in biblical teaching, it gains the clarity needed to evaluate cultural influences and determine which practices align with its convictions.

Healthy leadership encourages thoughtful engagement with the world while maintaining clear boundaries that protect the church's identity. The goal is not isolation from society but faithful witness within it. When the church retains its distinct character, it offers a visible example of lives shaped by the truth of the gospel.

By resisting uncritical cultural accommodation, the church preserves its ability to reflect the values of God's kingdom. Members are reminded that their identity is not defined by cultural trends but by their calling in Christ. This commitment strengthens the congregation's spiritual integrity and protects the church's culture from gradual erosion.

Chapter Fifteen
Financial and Structural Signals

The life of a church is not shaped only by teaching, worship, and fellowship. The structural and financial decisions made by leadership also send powerful signals about the congregation's priorities and convictions. These signals often influence the church's culture in ways members may not immediately recognize.

Every organization reveals its priorities through the way it allocates resources and organizes responsibilities. In the church, financial planning, facility decisions, staffing structures, and ministry investments all communicate what leadership believes to be most important. These choices shape how members interpret the congregation's mission and direction.

Financial stewardship provides one of the clearest examples of this principle. While statements of vision and mission describe the church's goals, the budget demonstrates how those goals are supported in practice. Resources directed toward discipleship, outreach, pastoral care, and ministry development reveal a commitment to the spiritual work of the church.

Structural decisions also shape the congregation's cultural environment. Leadership roles, ministry oversight, and organizational processes establish patterns that guide how the church functions. When structure aligns with the convictions and mission of the church, the congregation operates with clarity and stability.

However, when financial or structural decisions drift away from the church's stated priorities, confusion may develop. Members may struggle to understand the true direction of the congregation if leadership language and leadership actions appear inconsistent. Over time, this disconnect can erode trust and blur the church's cultural identity.

Healthy governance ensures that both financial stewardship and organizational structure remain aligned with the church's convictions. Decisions are made carefully, resources are allocated intentionally, and leadership responsibilities are clearly defined. These practices help reinforce the mission rather than distract from it.

This chapter explores how financial planning and organizational structure convey cultural signals within the church. By examining these patterns, leaders can better understand how their decisions shape the congregation's environment.

When financial and structural choices remain anchored to biblical conviction and mission clarity, they strengthen the cultural health of the church. Members can see that the congregation's practical operations support the spiritual purpose for which the church exists.

Budget as Conviction Revealed

The financial priorities of a church often reveal its deepest convictions. While written statements may describe the congregation's values and mission, the budget demonstrates how those convictions are translated into practical decisions. The allocation of resources reflects what the church believes is most important.

Matthew 6:21 (KJV) states, “For where your treasure is, there will your heart be also.” Jesus’ teaching highlights the close relationship between financial investment and personal commitment. What individuals or communities choose to support financially often reveals their true priorities.

This principle applies directly to the life of the church. Budgets determine which ministries receive resources, which initiatives are prioritized, and how the church prepares for future growth. Financial decisions shape the direction of the congregation and influence the activities that define its mission.

When financial planning aligns with the church's stated values and mission, the congregation gains clarity and unity. Members can see that the resources entrusted to the church are being used to advance the spiritual priorities they collectively affirm. The budget becomes a practical expression of shared conviction.

However, when financial decisions drift away from those convictions, the disconnect can influence the church's culture. Resources may begin to support activities that do not directly contribute to the mission. In other cases, essential ministries may remain underfunded while attention shifts toward less significant priorities.

Financial stewardship also communicates the seriousness with which leadership approaches the responsibilities entrusted to them. Careful budgeting, transparent reporting, and thoughtful planning demonstrate respect for the resources the congregation provides.

Leaders carry an important responsibility when developing and managing the church budget. Financial decisions should be guided by the same convictions that shape the church's values, vision, and mission. When those elements remain aligned, the budget reinforces the church's direction and purpose.

Over time, the church's financial structure becomes a visible signal of its priorities. Members observe where resources are directed and how decisions are made. When the budget consistently reflects the congregation's convictions, it strengthens trust and reinforces the church's cultural identity.

Production Spending Versus Discipleship Investment

Financial decisions within the church often reveal the priorities that shape its ministry focus. While many expenses are necessary for the operation of a congregation, the balance between different types of spending can communicate what the church values most. When resources are heavily directed toward presentation or production, the underlying mission of discipleship may receive less attention than intended.

Luke 12:15 (KJV) records a warning given by Jesus concerning misplaced priorities: "And he said unto them, Take heed, and beware of covetousness: for a man's life consisteth not in the abundance of the things which he possesseth." The principle expressed in this passage reminds believers that external abundance does not define spiritual health or success.

In modern church life, production spending typically refers to investments in stage equipment, lighting systems, sound technology, visual media, and other presentation elements. While these tools can support communication and worship, they can also become a dominant focus if they receive disproportionate attention and financial resources.

When the majority of resources are directed toward service delivery, the congregation may begin to view the gathering primarily as an event rather than as a community devoted to spiritual growth. The emphasis shifts from the depth of discipleship to the quality of the experience.

Discipleship investment, by contrast, focuses on the development of believers through teaching, mentoring, small group ministry, pastoral care, and spiritual formation. These areas may require fewer visible resources, yet they play a central role in the congregation's long-term spiritual maturity.

The challenge for leadership is not to eliminate all forms of production spending, but to ensure that such investments remain subordinate to the core mission of discipleship. Technology and presentation tools should support the church's work rather than define it.

When the church's financial priorities reflect commitment to spiritual development, the congregation gains a clearer understanding of its purpose. Members recognize that the church's goal extends beyond the quality of the weekly gathering to include the formation of faithful, mature disciples.

By maintaining a balance between operational needs and discipleship investment, leaders ensure that financial stewardship reinforces the church's mission. The allocation of resources becomes a visible expression of the church's commitment to spiritual growth rather than merely to presentation or production.

Compensation Transparency

Financial transparency within church leadership is important for maintaining trust between the congregation and those who oversee the ministry. While many aspects of church operations may remain administrative, compensation practices often convey important signals about integrity, stewardship, and accountability.

1 Timothy 5:18 (KJV) guides the support of those who labor in ministry: "For the scripture saith, Thou shalt not muzzle the ox that treadeth out the corn. And, The labourer is worthy of his reward." The passage affirms that those who dedicate their efforts to the work of ministry should be supported appropriately for their labor.

At the same time, Scripture consistently encourages responsible stewardship of resources entrusted to the church. Because financial contributions come from the faithful giving of members, leadership must exercise care in managing and distributing those resources. Compensation should reflect both fairness and accountability.

Transparency helps prevent misunderstanding within the congregation. When compensation structures are handled openly and with appropriate oversight, members gain confidence that financial decisions are being made responsibly. Clear governance reduces the possibility of suspicion, speculation, or confusion regarding the use of church resources.

This transparency does not necessarily require that every detail of compensation be publicly discussed in every setting. However, healthy churches often establish clear oversight structures, such as finance committees, elder boards, or independent review processes, to ensure that compensation decisions are made with integrity and balance.

These structures protect both the church and its leaders. Leaders are freed from the appearance of self-interest when compensation decisions are handled through appropriate governance. At the same time, the congregation is reassured that financial stewardship remains aligned with the church's mission.

Compensational transparency also reinforces the principle that ministry leadership is both a spiritual responsibility and a practical vocation. Those who serve the church deserve appropriate support, yet that support should always remain accountable to the community that provides it.

When compensation practices are managed with clarity and integrity, the church strengthens the culture of trust within the congregation. Financial stewardship reflects both biblical fairness and responsible governance, helping preserve the unity and credibility of the church's leadership.

Expansion Priorities

Periods of growth often lead churches to consider expansion. Increasing attendance, expanding ministries, and growing community engagement can create the need for additional space, staff, or resources. While expansion may represent a healthy development in a congregation's life, the priorities that guide it deserve careful examination.

Haggai 1:4 (KJV) presents a question directed to the people of Israel: "Is it time for you, O ye, to dwell in your cieled houses, and this house lie waste?" The prophet challenged the people to examine their priorities. While they had invested in their own comfort and development, the house of the Lord had been neglected. The passage highlights the importance of aligning priorities with the work God has entrusted to His people.

In the life of the church, expansion decisions communicate what leadership believes to be most important. The direction of financial investment, the types of facilities developed, and the ministries that receive additional resources all reflect the congregation's priorities.

When expansion focuses primarily on comfort, appearance, or prestige, the church may unintentionally shift attention away from its central mission. Facilities and programs can become ends in themselves rather than tools that serve the work of discipleship, teaching, and outreach.

Healthy expansion, by contrast, begins with a clear understanding of the church's mission. Leadership asks how additional space, staff, or resources will support the congregation's spiritual growth and the proclamation of the gospel. Expansion becomes a means of strengthening ministry rather than merely increasing visibility or convenience.

Financial stewardship also plays a significant role in these decisions. Major expansion projects require careful planning and long-term commitment from the congregation. Leaders must evaluate whether the proposed growth truly serves the church's mission or reflects a desire for larger facilities or more complex programs.

When expansion priorities remain anchored in the church's mission, the congregation benefits from greater capacity to serve its members and reach the surrounding community. New resources support discipleship, ministry development, and outreach efforts that advance the church's spiritual purpose.

In this way, expansion becomes an expression of faithful stewardship rather than an end in itself. By aligning growth with conviction and mission, church leaders ensure that structural development strengthens the church's work rather than distracts from it.

Stewardship and Witness

Financial stewardship within the church does more than support ministry operations. It also serves as a witness to the congregation and the broader community. The way a church manages its resources reflects the seriousness with which it approaches the responsibilities entrusted to it.

Luke 16:10 (KJV) teaches an important principle of faithfulness: “He that is faithful in that which is least is faithful also in much: and he that is unjust in the least is unjust also in much.” Jesus’ words emphasize that small matters of stewardship reveal the character and reliability of those who manage greater responsibilities.

In the context of the church, stewardship involves careful management of financial contributions, responsible planning, and transparent accountability. Members of the congregation give their resources with the expectation that those gifts will be used wisely for the advancement of the church’s mission.

When financial stewardship is handled with integrity, it strengthens trust within the congregation. Members gain confidence that their contributions support the work of ministry, outreach, discipleship, and community care. Faithful stewardship reinforces the unity of the church by demonstrating respect for the sacrifices made by those who give.

The witness of stewardship also extends beyond the congregation. Churches often interact with their surrounding communities through service projects, partnerships, and public presence. When financial decisions reflect responsibility and integrity, the church's reputation is strengthened.

Conversely, careless financial management can damage both internal trust and external credibility. Poor planning, lack of oversight, or unclear financial practices may create uncertainty within the congregation and weaken the church's public witness.

For this reason, leadership must approach financial stewardship with both diligence and humility. Budgets should reflect the church's mission, expenditures should be accountable, and financial practices should be conducted with transparency and integrity.

When stewardship is practiced faithfully, the church demonstrates that it values both spiritual responsibility and practical accountability. The management of resources becomes part of the church's testimony, showing that the community seeks to honor God not only in worship and teaching but also in the careful handling of what has been entrusted to it.

PART V
Stewarding Culture Under Biblical Authority

Culture within the church does not sustain itself automatically. Left unattended, cultural patterns gradually shift as new influences, preferences, and pressures emerge within the life of the congregation. Because culture reflects the community's repeated behaviors and priorities, it must be intentionally stewarded by leadership to remain aligned with biblical conviction.

Throughout this work, culture has been presented as the downstream result of leadership clarity. Values define conviction. Vision establishes direction. Mission defines the work of the church. Culture emerges as members repeatedly live out that mission under shared beliefs. Strategy and policy then guide and protect the environment that develops from those practices.

When these elements remain aligned, the church develops a stable and recognizable culture. Members understand what the church believes, how the mission is carried out, and the expected patterns of behavior within the community. The life of the congregation reflects the convictions that leadership has clearly communicated.

However, cultural stability requires ongoing stewardship. Leadership must continually reinforce the convictions that shape the church's mission and protect the structures that sustain its environment. Without intentional guidance, even healthy cultures can gradually drift as new habits and expectations take root.

Biblical authority provides the foundation for this stewardship. The church does not create its own standards of truth or morality. Rather, it receives guidance from Scripture, which establishes the principles that define both belief and practice within the community of faith.

This authority places a responsibility upon leaders to guide the church with faithfulness and humility. Leadership must continually return to Scripture's teachings when evaluating the direction of the congregation. Cultural patterns must be measured against biblical truth rather than against personal preference or cultural pressure.

Stewarding culture involves both vigilance and care. Leaders must remain attentive to the patterns that shape the life of the church, correcting drift when it appears and reinforcing the convictions that sustain unity. At the same time, this stewardship must be carried out with patience and wisdom, recognizing that cultural formation occurs gradually through consistent leadership.

The chapters that follow examine practical ways leaders can preserve cultural health within the church. By anchoring leadership decisions in biblical authority and maintaining alignment among conviction, mission, and practice, churches can cultivate environments that foster spiritual growth and faithful ministry.

When culture is stewarded under the authority of Scripture, the congregation gains both stability and clarity. Members understand the principles that guide their shared life, and the church remains faithful to the calling it has received.

Chapter Sixteen
Leadership Responsibility

Leadership carries significant responsibility for shaping and preserving the church's culture. While every member contributes to the congregation's environment, the direction and stability of that culture are largely influenced by those entrusted with spiritual oversight. The attitudes, decisions, and actions of leaders establish patterns that others often follow.

Throughout Scripture, leadership is consistently connected to stewardship. Leaders are not owners of the church but caretakers of the responsibilities God has entrusted to them. Their role is to guide the congregation with faithfulness, protecting both the spiritual health and the practical order of the community.

Because culture emerges from repeated behaviors and expectations, leadership example plays a powerful role in shaping the life of the church. Members observe how leaders speak, resolve conflict, approach worship, and respond to challenges. Over time, these examples help establish the norms that define the congregation's culture.

This influence places a particular weight on leadership conduct. When leaders model humility, conviction, discipline, and faithfulness, those qualities often become embedded within the broader community. Conversely, when leadership tolerates inconsistency or avoids difficult responsibilities, those patterns can also spread throughout the congregation.

Leadership responsibility also involves protecting doctrinal clarity and moral integrity. Churches depend on their leaders to teach Scripture faithfully, address error when it arises, and guide the congregation toward spiritual maturity. Without this guidance, confusion may develop regarding the beliefs and expectations that define the church.

At the same time, leadership responsibility should never be understood as authoritarian control. Biblical leadership emphasizes service, accountability, and humility. Leaders are called to guide the church while remaining submitted to the authority of Scripture and accountable to the community they serve.

The stewardship of culture requires both conviction and care. Leaders must remain attentive to the patterns developing within the congregation while also encouraging spiritual growth among its members. By reinforcing biblical principles and modeling faithful conduct, they help establish an environment where the church can thrive.

When leadership accepts this responsibility with humility and seriousness, the church's culture becomes more stable and resilient. The congregation gains clarity about its mission and convictions, and the community grows stronger through consistent and faithful guidance.

Pastoral Oversight

Pastoral oversight is one of the central responsibilities entrusted to spiritual leaders within the church. The role of a pastor extends beyond preaching and teaching. It includes the care, guidance, and protection of the congregation entrusted to their leadership. Through this oversight, pastors help ensure that the life of the church remains aligned with biblical conviction and spiritual purpose.

1 Peter 5:2 (KJV) instructs church leaders with these words: "Feed the flock of God which is among you, taking the oversight

thereof, not by constraint, but willingly; not for filthy lucre, but of a ready mind." The passage presents pastoral leadership as a form of stewardship carried out willingly and faithfully for the congregation's benefit.

Pastoral oversight involves both spiritual and practical responsibilities. Pastors guide the church through the teaching of Scripture, helping members understand and apply biblical truth in their daily lives. They also remain attentive to the needs of the congregation, offering counsel, encouragement, and prayer to those under their care.

This oversight also includes protecting the church from influences that could weaken its spiritual health. Pastors must remain attentive to doctrinal accuracy, moral integrity, and the congregation's overall direction. When challenges arise, pastoral leadership provides clarity and guidance so that the church can respond wisely.

Oversight responsibility requires consistent presence and attentiveness. Pastors must remain connected to the congregation's life to understand its needs and concerns. Through personal interaction, observation, and prayerful reflection, they gain insight into the church's spiritual condition.

At the same time, pastoral oversight is not exercised in isolation. Healthy churches often share leadership responsibilities among elders, ministry leaders, and other trusted individuals who help guide the congregation. This shared leadership helps maintain balance and accountability while strengthening the care provided to members.

When pastoral oversight is exercised faithfully, the congregation experiences stability and guidance. Members understand that leadership is attentive to both their spiritual growth and the church's overall direction. This environment helps preserve unity and encourages continued maturity within the body of Christ.

Through careful oversight, pastors help ensure that the convictions, mission, and culture of the church remain aligned with Scripture's teachings. Their leadership serves as a steady influence, protecting the congregation's spiritual health and guiding it toward faithful ministry.

Board and Elder Accountability

Healthy church governance requires accountability among those entrusted with leadership. While pastoral oversight provides spiritual direction, the presence of qualified elders or governing boards helps ensure that leadership remains balanced, transparent, and faithful to the church's mission. Shared leadership structures provide stability and protect the congregation from the dangers of isolated authority.

Titus 1:5–9 (KJV) describes the appointment of elders within the early church and outlines the qualifications required for those who serve in positions of oversight. These qualifications emphasize character, self-control, doctrinal integrity, and the ability to teach sound doctrine. The passage highlights that leadership within the church must be grounded in both spiritual maturity and moral responsibility.

Boards and elders serve as a system of accountability that supports pastoral leadership while also overseeing the broader life of the church. Their role is not to compete with pastoral authority but to strengthen it through shared responsibility and wise counsel. Together, these leaders help guide the congregation in matters of doctrine, governance, and stewardship.

Accountability among leaders protects both the church and those who serve within it. When decisions are made collectively rather than individually, the risk of personal bias or error is reduced. Shared leadership encourages careful discussion, prayerful reflection, and thoughtful decision-making before significant actions are taken.

This structure also provides a safeguard against leadership drift. If the direction of the church moves away from its stated convictions, a healthy board or elder body can help address the issue and restore alignment. Accountability ensures that leadership remains anchored to the values, vision, and mission that define the congregation.

Effective boards and elder groups operate with clarity regarding their responsibilities. Members should understand their role in providing spiritual oversight, maintaining doctrinal integrity, and supporting the church's overall mission. When these responsibilities are carried out faithfully, the leadership structure functions as a stabilizing influence within the congregation.

At the same time, accountability requires humility among all leaders involved. Pastors, elders, and board members must remain open to correction, willing to listen to one another, and committed to the shared responsibility of guiding the church. Leadership that values mutual accountability fosters trust within the congregation.

When boards and elders function according to biblical principles, they strengthen the church's governance and support the work of pastoral leadership. Their presence helps maintain clarity, integrity, and unity within the congregation while protecting the church from instability or unchecked authority.

Policy as Protective Structure

Healthy governance within the church requires more than good intentions. Clear structures must exist to guide decision-making, protect the church's mission, and ensure consistency in leadership practices. Policy serves as one of the primary tools through which these structures are established and maintained.

Nehemiah 4:9 (KJV) illustrates a balanced approach to leadership during a time of difficulty: "Nevertheless we made our prayer unto our God, and set a watch against them day and night." The people of Jerusalem combined spiritual dependence with practical preparation. Prayer demonstrated their trust in God, while the watch protected the work they were carrying out.

This principle applies to the church's governance. Spiritual leadership depends on prayer, biblical teaching, and the guidance of the Holy Spirit. At the same time, practical structures are necessary to protect the integrity of the church's mission. Policy provides the framework for consistently carrying out these responsibilities.

Policies establish clear expectations for leadership behavior, financial stewardship, ministry oversight, and decision-making processes. By defining how certain matters are handled, policies reduce confusion and help ensure that actions remain aligned with the church's convictions and mission.

Without such structures, leadership decisions may become inconsistent or reactive. Situations may be handled differently depending on the individuals involved or the pressures present at the moment. Over time, this inconsistency can weaken trust and create uncertainty within the congregation.

Policy also protects the church during moments of conflict or difficulty. When expectations are clearly established in advance, leaders can respond to challenges with greater clarity and fairness. The presence of agreed-upon procedures helps guide decisions even when emotions or disagreements arise.

It is important to recognize that policy does not replace spiritual leadership. Structures exist to support the church's mission, not to control it. Effective policies serve as guardrails that help preserve alignment with the church's convictions while allowing leaders to fulfill their responsibilities faithfully.

When policy is carefully developed and consistently followed, it strengthens the church's stability. Members understand how decisions are made, leaders operate within clear boundaries, and the congregation's mission remains protected. Through this protective structure, governance helps preserve both the integrity and the unity of the church.

Hiring and Cultural Continuity

The individuals selected for leadership and ministry roles play a significant role in shaping a church's culture. Every hiring decision introduces a new voice, a new influence, and a new example within the life of the congregation. Because culture develops through repeated behaviors and shared convictions, the people entrusted with leadership responsibilities help determine whether that culture remains stable or begins to shift.

2 Timothy 2:2 (KJV) emphasizes the importance of careful selection and transmission of responsibility: "And the things that thou hast heard of me among many witnesses, the same commit thou to faithful men, who shall be able to teach others also." Paul instructs Timothy to pass leadership responsibility to individuals who demonstrate faithfulness and the ability to continue teaching others. The passage highlights the importance of continuity in leadership and doctrine.

Within the church, hiring decisions should therefore consider more than professional ability or ministry experience. While skills and qualifications are important, leaders must also evaluate whether potential staff members understand and share the convictions that shape the congregation's culture.

When new leaders are chosen without careful attention to cultural alignment, the church's direction can gradually shift. Even well-intentioned individuals may introduce different priorities, leadership styles, or theological emphases that alter the congregation's environment. Over time, these differences can create confusion about the church's identity and mission.

By contrast, when hiring decisions intentionally prioritize cultural alignment, new leaders strengthen the continuity of the church's mission. Individuals who share the same convictions and vision reinforce the patterns already present within the congregation. Their leadership supports the stability of the culture rather than redirecting it.

This process requires thoughtful evaluation and clear communication. Potential leaders should understand the church's values, vision, and mission before accepting positions of responsibility. Likewise, hiring teams must carefully assess whether candidates demonstrate both the character and the commitment necessary to sustain those convictions.

Hiring also provides an opportunity for long-term investment in the church's future. By selecting individuals who are capable of teaching, mentoring, and developing others, leadership creates a cycle of continued growth and stability within the congregation.

When hiring decisions are guided by both qualification and conviction, the church preserves its cultural continuity across generations of leadership. New leaders contribute fresh energy and perspective while remaining anchored to the principles that define the church's identity and mission.

Promotion and Reinforcement

Leadership promotion within the church communicates powerful cultural signals to the congregation. When individuals are elevated to positions of influence, the church observes not only the appointment itself but also the qualities that leadership has chosen to recognize and affirm. In this way, promotion reinforces the standards and expectations that shape the church's culture.

1 Timothy 3:1–7 (KJV) provides clear guidance regarding the qualifications required for those who serve in positions of oversight. The passage describes characteristics such as integrity, self-control, faithfulness in family life, sound judgment, and a good reputation among those outside the church. These qualifications emphasize that leadership in the church is grounded primarily in character rather than in popularity or personal ambition.

Promotion functions as a form of cultural reinforcement. When individuals who demonstrate biblical character and faithful service are entrusted with greater responsibility, the congregation receives a clear message about what qualities the church values most. Members see that spiritual maturity, humility, and integrity are the standards by which leadership is recognized.

Conversely, when promotions are based primarily on visibility, influence, or personal relationships, the cultural message becomes less clear. Members may struggle to understand the criteria guiding leadership decisions. Over time, such patterns can erode confidence in the leadership structure and create confusion about expectations for spiritual leadership.

Careful promotion decisions help preserve the integrity of the church's leadership culture. Leaders must evaluate whether individuals have demonstrated consistent faithfulness in smaller responsibilities before entrusting them with greater authority. This process reflects the biblical principle that leadership should grow from proven character and sustained service.

Promotion also reinforces the connection between responsibility and accountability. Those who are entrusted with leadership roles are expected to model the same convictions and behaviors that the church seeks to cultivate throughout the congregation. Their example influences both the culture of leadership and the broader life of the church.

When promotion practices align with biblical qualifications, the church strengthens its leadership culture. Members gain confidence that those placed in positions of authority reflect the convictions and character expected of spiritual leaders.

Through careful and principled promotion, leadership helps preserve the cultural health of the church. The congregation sees that responsibility is entrusted to those who demonstrate faithfulness, thereby reinforcing the values and standards that guide the community's life.

Chapter Seventeen
Discipline as Cultural Protection

Discipline within the church is often misunderstood. In many settings, the word carries negative connotations associated with punishment or exclusion. Yet within the biblical framework, discipline serves a protective and restorative purpose. Its primary goal is not condemnation but the preservation of spiritual health within the community of faith.

Throughout Scripture, discipline serves to maintain the integrity of God's people. When harmful behavior or persistent sin is addressed with wisdom and care, the church is protected from patterns that could weaken its convictions and disrupt its unity. Discipline serves as a safeguard for the congregation's cultural and spiritual environment.

Repeated behaviors and expectations shape church culture. When those expectations are consistently upheld, members understand the standards that guide the community. However, when serious issues remain unaddressed, confusion may arise regarding what the church truly believes and practices.

In such moments, discipline provides clarity. By addressing behavior that conflicts with biblical teaching, leadership reinforces the convictions that define the church's identity. Members are reminded that the church is committed to living according to the principles of Scripture rather than adapting its standards to shifting circumstances.

Discipline also serves a restorative purpose for the individual involved. Scripture consistently presents correction as an opportunity for repentance and reconciliation. When carried out with humility and compassion, discipline seeks to guide individuals back toward spiritual health rather than simply removing them from the community.

For this reason, discipline must be practiced with great care. Leaders must approach such situations with prayer, patience, and a sincere desire for restoration. The goal is always the spiritual well-being of the individual and the protection of the congregation.

Avoiding discipline may appear to preserve peace in the short term, but it often allows deeper problems to develop beneath the surface. Over time, unresolved issues can weaken trust and alter the expectations that shape the life of the church.

When discipline is practiced according to biblical principles, it strengthens the church's culture rather than harming it. Members see that the community takes both holiness and restoration seriously. Leadership demonstrates its commitment to protecting the integrity of the church while also extending grace to those who seek repentance.

In this way, discipline functions as a form of cultural protection. It preserves the convictions that guide the church, supports the unity of the congregation, and encourages believers to pursue lives that reflect the character of Christ.

Matthew 18 and Ordered Correction

Scripture provides clear guidance for how correction should occur within the church. Rather than allowing conflict to develop without direction, the Bible outlines an ordered process that protects both the individual involved and the unity of the congregation. One of the most well-known instructions for addressing wrongdoing appears in the words of Jesus recorded in Matthew 18.

Matthew 18:15–17 (KJV) states: "Moreover if thy brother shall trespass against thee, go and tell him his fault between thee and him alone: if he shall hear thee, thou hast gained thy brother. But if he will not hear thee, then take with thee one or two more, that in the mouth of two or three witnesses every word may be established. And if he shall neglect to hear them, tell it unto the church: but if he neglect to hear the church, let him be unto thee as an heathen man and a publican."

This passage establishes a clear pattern for addressing conflict and sin within the Christian community. Correction begins privately, allowing the matter to be resolved without unnecessary public exposure. The goal at this stage is restoration. When individuals are willing to listen and respond with humility, reconciliation can occur quickly and quietly.

If the issue cannot be resolved privately, the process moves to a second stage involving additional witnesses. The presence of others helps confirm the facts of the situation and provides accountability for both parties. This step ensures that correction is handled fairly and responsibly.

Only when these earlier efforts fail does the matter move to the wider church community. Even at this stage, the purpose remains restoration rather than punishment. The church's involvement reflects the seriousness of the situation and encourages the individual to reconsider their actions.

The final stage described by Jesus recognizes that persistent refusal to respond to correction may require separation from the church's fellowship. Such a decision is not intended to express hostility but to acknowledge that the individual has chosen to reject the community's guidance.

This ordered process demonstrates both wisdom and care. By progressing through clear stages, the church avoids impulsive or harsh responses while still addressing serious issues when necessary. Each step provides opportunities for repentance and reconciliation.

When churches follow this biblical pattern, discipline becomes both fair and restorative. Members understand that correction will be handled with integrity and patience. At the same time, the congregation recognizes that harmful behavior will not be ignored.

In this way, the instructions of Matthew 18 provide a structured approach to correction that protects both the unity and the cultural health of the church. Through ordered correction, the church maintains its commitment to truth while continually seeking restoration for those who have gone astray.

1 Corinthians 5 and Congregational Integrity

The integrity of a church community depends on its willingness to address serious sin when it appears within the congregation. While correction should always be approached with humility and care, Scripture teaches that the church cannot ignore conduct that openly contradicts the moral standards it professes to uphold. When such situations arise, leadership must act to protect the community's spiritual health.

1 Corinthians 5 describes a case in which a serious moral violation had been tolerated within the church at Corinth. Rather than confronting the issue, the congregation had allowed the situation to continue without correction. The apostle Paul responded with strong concern, instructing the church to address the matter directly.

Paul's warning emphasized that the tolerance of open wrongdoing does not remain isolated. He compared the situation to leaven spreading through dough, explaining that even a small amount can influence the entire mixture. In the same way, unaddressed sin can gradually influence the expectations and behavior of the wider congregation.

The concern in this passage is not simply the conduct of one individual but the integrity of the entire church. When a congregation refuses to address clear moral violations, it risks sending a message that its convictions are optional. Members may begin to question whether the church truly believes the standards it claims to uphold.

Discipline in this context serves both protective and restorative purposes. By confronting serious wrongdoing, the church affirms its commitment to biblical holiness. At the same time, the correction process is intended to lead the individual toward repentance and restoration.

Paul's instruction demonstrates that congregational integrity requires action when necessary. Ignoring such issues does not preserve unity; rather, it weakens the church's moral clarity and allows harmful patterns to spread within the community.

Leadership must therefore approach situations of serious misconduct with both wisdom and courage. Discipline should be exercised carefully, with a desire to restore rather than condemn. Yet the responsibility to protect the integrity of the church cannot be neglected.

When correction is carried out faithfully, the church preserves the cultural standards that define its life together. Members see that the congregation remains committed to living according to Scripture's teachings. In this way, discipline strengthens the integrity of the community and reinforces the convictions that guide its mission.

Restoration and Accountability

The purpose of discipline within the church is not punishment but restoration. When individuals fall into sin or harmful patterns of behavior, the goal of correction is to guide them back toward spiritual health and renewed fellowship with the community. Biblical discipline combines accountability with compassion.

Galatians 6:1 (KJV) provides clear instruction regarding this process: "Brethren, if a man be overtaken in a fault, ye which are spiritual, restore such an one in the spirit of meekness; considering thyself, lest thou also be tempted." The passage emphasizes both the responsibility to address wrongdoing and the humility required when doing so. Restoration must be pursued with gentleness and self-awareness.

Accountability plays an essential role in this process. Without honest acknowledgment of wrongdoing, restoration cannot occur. Individuals must be willing to recognize the harm caused by their actions and take steps toward repentance and change. Accountability provides the structure that makes this transformation possible.

At the same time, those involved in the correction process must approach the situation with humility. The instruction to consider one's own vulnerability reminds believers that all are capable of failure. Correction should therefore never be carried out with pride or condemnation.

Healthy churches maintain both accountability and compassion in balance. When discipline occurs, the congregation understands that the purpose is not exclusion but healing. Members see that the church takes sin seriously while also extending grace to those who seek repentance.

Restoration also requires practical support. Individuals who are seeking to change often benefit from guidance, mentorship, and encouragement from trusted members of the church. These relationships help reinforce new patterns of behavior and strengthen spiritual growth.

Through this combination of accountability and support, restoration becomes possible. The individual is not abandoned but guided toward renewed fellowship and spiritual maturity. The church community benefits as well, seeing that correction leads toward healing rather than permanent separation.

When restoration and accountability function together, discipline fulfills its biblical purpose. The integrity of the church is preserved, individuals are allowed to return to healthy fellowship, and the congregation continues to reflect the grace and truth that define the life of the Christian community.

Mercy Without Permissiveness

The church is called to demonstrate mercy toward those who struggle with sin and spiritual weakness. Mercy reflects the compassion of Christ and reminds believers that restoration remains possible even when individuals have wandered from the path of faithfulness. At the same time, Scripture teaches that mercy must never become permissiveness. Compassion does not require the acceptance of behavior that contradicts biblical truth.

Jude 22–23 (KJV) provides a balanced instruction for responding to those who are struggling: "And of some have compassion, making a difference: And others save with fear, pulling them out of the fire; hating even the garment spotted by the flesh." The passage recognizes that different situations require different responses. Some individuals respond to gentle compassion, while others require stronger intervention to prevent further harm.

This distinction highlights the need for discernment in church leadership. Mercy should always guide the spirit in which correction occurs, yet leaders must also recognize when firm boundaries are necessary. Allowing destructive behavior to continue unchecked may appear compassionate in the moment, but it ultimately harms both the individual and the community.

Permissiveness often develops when leaders confuse compassion with avoiding difficult conversations. Out of a desire to show grace, correction may be postponed or avoided entirely. Over time, however, this reluctance can allow harmful patterns to take root within the church.

Biblical mercy addresses sin honestly while still extending the possibility of restoration. Leaders speak truth clearly, establish appropriate boundaries, and invite individuals to return to a healthier path. Mercy works alongside accountability rather than replacing it.

This balance protects both the individual and the congregation. Those who are struggling receive the opportunity for restoration, while the church maintains its commitment to biblical conviction. Members understand that compassion within the church does not require abandoning moral clarity.

When mercy and accountability remain properly aligned, the church reflects both the grace and the holiness of God. Individuals encounter a community that is willing to offer forgiveness and support while still maintaining the standards that define faithful Christian living.

In this way, mercy without permissiveness becomes an essential element of cultural protection within the church. Leaders demonstrate compassion while preserving the integrity of the congregation, ensuring that grace and truth continue to guide the community's life.

Distinction Between Struggle and Normalization

Within the life of the church, it is important to distinguish between personal struggle and the normalization of sin. Every believer experiences areas of weakness and ongoing spiritual growth. Scripture recognizes that Christians continue to face temptation and must continually pursue repentance and transformation. The presence of struggle does not remove a person from the life of the church.

Romans 6:1–2 (KJV) addresses this issue directly: "What shall we say then? Shall we continue in sin, that grace may abound? God forbid. How shall we, that are dead to sin, live any longer therein?" Paul emphasizes that the grace of God is not a justification for continuing in patterns of sin. Salvation calls believers toward a new life shaped by righteousness.

This distinction between struggle and normalization is essential for maintaining both compassion and integrity within the church. Struggle refers to situations in which a believer recognizes wrongdoing, seeks repentance, and desires to grow in obedience to God. In such cases, the church provides encouragement, accountability, and support for spiritual growth.

Normalization, by contrast, occurs when behavior that contradicts biblical teaching is no longer considered to require repentance or change. When sin becomes accepted or defended within the community, the church's moral clarity begins to weaken. Over time, members may struggle to distinguish between biblical conviction and cultural preference.

Leaders must approach these situations with discernment. Individuals who are struggling with sin should encounter patience, guidance, and restoration. The church serves as a place where believers help one another pursue spiritual maturity.

However, when behavior becomes openly defended or presented as acceptable within the life of the church, leadership must respond with clarity. Allowing normalization of sin communicates that the convictions of the church are optional. Such patterns can gradually reshape the congregation's culture.

By maintaining this distinction, the church preserves both grace and truth. Members understand that personal struggle does not remove them from the community of faith, yet they also recognize that the church remains committed to the moral teachings of Scripture.

When struggle is met with compassion and normalization is addressed with conviction, the church's culture remains both restorative and faithful. The congregation becomes a place where believers are encouraged to grow in holiness while receiving the support necessary to pursue that transformation.

Chapter Eighteen Measuring Cultural Alignment

Culture within the church develops gradually through repeated behaviors, shared expectations, and the influence of leadership decisions. Because culture is often experienced rather than formally documented, it can be difficult for leaders to recognize when drift begins. For this reason, thoughtful evaluation is necessary to determine whether the congregation's lived culture remains aligned with its stated convictions.

Cultural alignment exists when the church's behaviors, priorities, and practices consistently reflect its declared values, vision, and mission. Members should be able to observe clear connections between what the church says it believes and how the church actually operates. When this alignment is present, the congregation experiences clarity and unity.

However, alignment can weaken over time if leadership does not periodically evaluate the church's cultural environment. Leadership changes, increased attendance, new ministry initiatives, and shifting cultural pressures can all influence the congregation's behavior. Without intentional reflection, these influences may gradually reshape the church's environment.

Measuring cultural alignment does not require complex systems or extensive data collection. Instead, it begins with careful observation and honest evaluation of the patterns that shape the congregation's life. Leaders must consider whether the church's daily practices reinforce the convictions they publicly proclaim.

Several indicators can reveal the level of cultural alignment within a church. The language used by leaders and members, the priorities reflected in ministry activities, the allocation of financial resources, and the behavior encouraged or tolerated within the congregation all provide valuable insight into the church's true culture.

When these indicators reflect the church's stated convictions, leadership can be confident that the congregation is moving in the intended direction. The mission of the church becomes visible not only in official statements but also in the everyday life of the community.

Conversely, when a gap begins to appear between stated convictions and lived behavior, leadership must take notice. Such gaps often signal the early stages of cultural drift. Addressing these issues early allows leaders to reinforce alignment before deeper instability develops.

Regular evaluation also encourages accountability within leadership. By examining the patterns that shape the congregation, leaders can determine whether their decisions, structures, and policies are strengthening the church's mission or unintentionally redirecting it.

Measuring cultural alignment becomes an important act of stewardship. Through careful observation and honest reflection, leaders ensure that the church continues to reflect the convictions that define its identity.

When cultural alignment is consistently examined and reinforced, the church remains stable in both belief and practice. The congregation grows in unity, and the church's mission continues to advance with clarity and purpose.

Crisis Response

Moments of crisis often reveal the true condition of a church's culture. While everyday ministry activities may reflect the normal patterns of congregational life, unexpected challenges can expose underlying attitudes, priorities, and leadership practices. During such moments, the responses of both leaders and members provide valuable insight into the church's cultural environment.

Mark 4:40 (KJV) records Jesus addressing the disciples during a storm on the Sea of Galilee: "And he said unto them, Why are ye so fearful? how is it that ye have no faith?" The disciples had witnessed many demonstrations of Christ's power, yet their response in the storm revealed the depth of their trust and understanding. The crisis exposed the gap between what they had experienced and what they fully believed.

A similar pattern can occur within the church. During seasons of stability, cultural weaknesses may remain hidden beneath routine activity. However, when a crisis arises, the behaviors and attitudes of leadership and members quickly reveal the strength or weakness of the church's underlying convictions.

Crises may take many forms, including financial difficulties, leadership conflicts, public controversies, or sudden changes in attendance or resources. These moments place pressure on the structures and relationships within the church, often exposing patterns that were previously unnoticed.

Leadership responses during a crisis are particularly significant. When leaders remain calm, principled, and guided by biblical conviction, they reinforce stability within the congregation. Members observe that leadership decisions are grounded in faith and clarity rather than in fear or in reactive impulses.

Conversely, when leadership responds to a crisis with confusion, inconsistency, or avoidance, the congregation may experience uncertainty about the church's direction. Members may begin to question whether the church's convictions truly guide its decisions in difficult moments.

Crisis serves as an informal test of cultural alignment. It reveals whether the church's values, vision, and mission are deeply embedded in the congregation's life or merely expressed through leadership language.

While crises are rarely welcomed, they can provide valuable opportunities for reflection and growth. Leaders who carefully evaluate their responses to crises can gain insight into areas where the church's culture may need strengthening.

By learning from these moments, leadership can reinforce the convictions and structures that support cultural stability. Over time, the congregation becomes more resilient, better prepared to face challenges while remaining anchored to the mission and principles that define its identity.

Conflict Patterns

Conflict is an unavoidable part of human relationships, including within the life of the church. Differences in perspective, personality, and experience can sometimes produce disagreement among members. While conflict itself is not unusual, the patterns through which a church handles disagreement reveal important aspects of its culture.

Philippians 4:2–3 (KJV) records Paul addressing a conflict between two individuals within the church at Philippi: "I beseech Euodias, and beseech Syntyche, that they agree in the Lord. And I intreat thee also, true yokefellow, help those women which laboured with me in the gospel…" The passage shows that even committed believers can experience disagreement. At the same time, it demonstrates the importance of resolving conflict in a way that preserves unity within the church.

The way conflict unfolds within a congregation provides valuable insight into its cultural environment. In healthy churches, disagreements are addressed openly, respectfully, and with a desire for reconciliation. Members seek understanding rather than personal victory, and leaders guide conversations toward restoration and unity.

In other situations, conflict may develop through unhealthy patterns. Disagreements may be avoided rather than addressed, allowing tension to grow beneath the surface. In some cases, members may form factions or engage in indirect communication through gossip or criticism. These patterns weaken trust and create instability within the congregation.

Leadership plays an important role in shaping how conflict is handled. When leaders model humility, patience, and biblical principles in their own interactions, they help establish expectations for the rest of the church. Members observe that disagreement can be addressed without hostility or division.

Conflict patterns function as an indicator of cultural alignment. A church grounded in biblical conviction will typically approach disagreement with a commitment to reconciliation and mutual respect. Members recognize that unity within the body of Christ requires effort, humility, and forgiveness.

When leaders observe recurring patterns of unresolved conflict, it may signal the need for cultural reinforcement. Teaching on biblical reconciliation, clear communication from leadership, and the consistent application of scriptural principles can help restore healthier patterns of interaction.

By examining how conflict is handled within the congregation, leaders gain insight into the deeper cultural dynamics of the church. These observations help them strengthen unity and ensure that relationships within the church reflect the values and convictions the congregation seeks to uphold.

Financial Decisions

Financial decisions within the church provide an important window into the congregation's priorities and convictions. While sermons and written statements may describe the church's mission and values, financial choices demonstrate how those commitments are put into practice in daily governance. Resource allocation reveals what leadership considers worthy of investment.

Luke 16:10 (KJV) teaches a principle that applies directly to stewardship: "He that is faithful in that which is least is faithful also in much: and he that is unjust in the least is unjust also in much." Jesus emphasizes that faithfulness in small matters reflects the character of those entrusted with greater responsibility. In the life of the church, financial stewardship provides a visible expression of that faithfulness.

Budgets, expenditures, and long-term financial planning all communicate cultural signals to the congregation. When resources are directed toward ministries that support discipleship, teaching, outreach, and pastoral care, members see that the church is investing in its spiritual mission. Financial alignment strengthens the connection between the church's stated convictions and its practical operations.

Conversely, financial decisions that appear disconnected from the church's mission can raise important questions. If significant resources are directed toward priorities that do not clearly support the church's spiritual work, members may struggle to understand how those decisions relate to the congregation's values and mission.

Financial decisions also reflect leadership accountability. Transparent processes, careful oversight, and responsible stewardship demonstrate respect for the resources entrusted to the church by its members. These practices strengthen trust within the congregation and reinforce the credibility of leadership.

For this reason, examining financial patterns can provide insight into the level of cultural alignment within the church. Leaders can ask whether the budget aligns with the church's values, vision, and mission statements. If inconsistencies arise, they may signal areas that need cultural reinforcement.

Financial evaluation should not focus solely on numerical results but also on the direction of investment. Resources should consistently support the spiritual formation of the congregation and the advancement of the church's mission.

When financial decisions align with biblical conviction and organizational purpose, they strengthen the church's cultural stability. Members recognize that stewardship is being practiced faithfully, and the practical operations of the church continue to support the mission it seeks to fulfill.

Platform Visibility

Those who are given visible roles within the life of the church often communicate important cultural signals to the congregation. The individuals who appear on the platform, lead ministries, or represent the church publicly influence how members understand leadership, responsibility, and spiritual maturity. Platform visibility carries a level of influence that extends beyond the specific task being performed.

1 Timothy 5:22 (KJV) provides an important caution regarding leadership recognition: "Lay hands suddenly on no man, neither be partaker of other men's sins: keep thyself pure." The instruction reminds leaders to exercise care when affirming individuals for positions of influence. Public endorsement should follow careful evaluation of character and spiritual maturity.

Within the church, the platform represents more than a physical location. It symbolizes trust, responsibility, and spiritual influence. Members often assume that individuals who occupy visible roles have been recognized by leadership as examples worthy of respect and imitation.

For this reason, decisions regarding platform visibility require thoughtful consideration. When individuals are placed in prominent roles without careful evaluation, the congregation may receive mixed signals regarding the standards expected of leaders.

Visibility can unintentionally communicate endorsement of behavior or character that has not yet been tested.

At the same time, the careful selection of those who serve in visible roles reinforces the church's cultural values. When individuals known for humility, faithfulness, and spiritual maturity are entrusted with public responsibility, the congregation sees those qualities affirmed as the standard for leadership.

Platform visibility also shapes expectations for participation within the church. Members often look to those who lead worship, teach, or assist in public ministry as examples of how believers should live and serve. Their conduct contributes to the congregation's overall tone.

Leaders must therefore approach these decisions with wisdom and patience. Public roles should reflect the convictions and character that leadership desires to reinforce within the church's culture. Careful evaluation protects both the individual and the congregation from the consequences of premature recognition.

When platform visibility is managed responsibly, it strengthens cultural alignment within the church. Members observe that leadership influence is entrusted to those who demonstrate faithful character, reinforcing the values that guide the life of the congregation.

Repeated Behavioral Observation

Culture within the church is most clearly revealed through repeated patterns of behavior. While individual actions may occasionally reflect temporary circumstances, consistent patterns over time provide a clearer picture of the congregation's true environment. Observing these patterns allows leaders to evaluate whether the church's culture remains aligned with its stated convictions.

Matthew 7:16 (KJV) presents a simple but powerful principle: "Ye shall know them by their fruits. Do men gather grapes of thorns, or figs of thistles?" Jesus used the image of fruit to illustrate that the true nature of something is revealed by the results it consistently produces. Character and belief eventually become visible through behavior.

This principle applies not only to individuals but also to the life of a congregation. The repeated behaviors of leaders and members reveal the church's actual priorities. Over time, patterns of speech, decision-making, participation, and ministry involvement demonstrate what the church truly values.

For this reason, cultural evaluation should focus on consistent observation rather than isolated incidents. A single moment of disagreement, confusion, or failure does not necessarily define a church's character. However, when similar behaviors recur, they often indicate deeper patterns within the congregation's culture.

Leaders who pay attention to these patterns gain valuable insight into the church's health. For example, recurring patterns of hospitality, humility, and service may indicate that the congregation is living out its stated convictions. On the other hand, repeated patterns of division, neglect, or inconsistency may reveal areas that require cultural reinforcement.

Repeated observation also helps leaders evaluate whether policies, structures, and teaching are producing the intended results. If the behaviors encouraged by leadership appear consistently within the congregation, it suggests that the church's values and mission are being effectively communicated.

Conversely, when the congregation's behavior differs significantly from the church's stated convictions, leadership may need to examine whether its guidance and structures reinforce the desired culture.

By observing repeated behavioral patterns, leaders can use a practical method to measure cultural alignment. The everyday actions of the congregation reveal whether the church is truly living according to its convictions.

When observable patterns of behavior reflect biblical values and the church’s mission, leaders can be confident that the congregation's culture remains healthy and aligned with its purpose.

Chapter Nineteen
Public Witness and Cultural Integrity

The culture of a church does not remain confined within its walls. The behavior, priorities, and decisions of the congregation inevitably become visible to the surrounding community. For this reason, the church's internal culture directly influences its public witness. What the church practices privately will eventually shape how it is perceived publicly.

Throughout Scripture, the people of God are called to live in a manner that reflects the character of the One they represent. The church exists not only as a gathering for worship and discipleship but also as a visible testimony to the transforming work of Christ. The integrity of that testimony depends on the consistency between belief and behavior.

Public witness is therefore closely connected to cultural integrity. When the convictions of the church are consistently reflected in its conduct, the surrounding community can observe a clear example of faith lived out in practice. Members demonstrate the values they proclaim through their speech, relationships, stewardship, and service.

Conversely, when a church's internal culture conflicts with its stated beliefs, that inconsistency often becomes apparent beyond the congregation. Conflicts, leadership failures, financial mismanagement, or moral compromise can undermine the church's message in the community's eyes.

For this reason, cultural stewardship is not only an internal concern but also a matter of public responsibility. The church's reputation influences how the gospel message is received by those who observe it from the outside. Integrity within the congregation strengthens the credibility of its witness.

Leadership plays a key role in preserving this integrity. By maintaining clear convictions, practicing faithful stewardship, and addressing issues that threaten the unity or character of the church, leaders help ensure that the congregation reflects the values it proclaims.

Members also contribute to this witness through their daily lives. The culture of the church is expressed through how believers interact with one another and with the broader community. Acts of kindness, humility, service, and integrity demonstrate the practical implications of the gospel.

A church that preserves cultural integrity becomes a visible example of faith in action. The community observes not only what the church teaches but also how its members live and relate to one another.

When internal culture and public witness remain aligned, the church's message gains credibility and clarity. The congregation reflects the character of Christ both within its fellowship and in the presence of the world it seeks to serve.

Internal Culture as External Testimony

The internal life of the church inevitably becomes visible to those outside the congregation. While a church may carefully craft public messaging, the most powerful testimony to the surrounding community is the lived culture of its members. How believers treat one another, resolve conflict, and demonstrate unity becomes a visible reflection of the faith they profess.

Jesus directly connected the internal relationships of His followers with the credibility of their witness to the world. In John 13:35 (KJV), He declared, “By this shall all men know that ye are my disciples, if ye have love one to another.” The distinguishing mark of Christian discipleship was not intended to be organizational structure, public reputation, or external programs. Instead, it was the observable love shared among believers.

This principle reveals that the church's internal culture serves as an external testimony. When members demonstrate patience, humility, forgiveness, and genuine care for one another, those outside the church witness the transforming influence of the gospel in practical form. Such relationships become a living example of Christ’s work within the community of believers.

However, when internal relationships are marked by division, hostility, or persistent conflict, the public testimony of the church is weakened. Observers may question the sincerity of the message proclaimed if the congregation's life does not reflect the character of Christ.

For this reason, leadership must view the church's internal culture as part of its public mission. Teaching, governance, and discipleship should reinforce behaviors that promote unity, mutual respect, and genuine love among members. These qualities strengthen both the congregation's health and the credibility of its witness.

The daily interactions within the church carry significant weight. Conversations, acts of service, moments of forgiveness, and shared burdens all contribute to the culture that the church displays before the world.

When believers consistently demonstrate Christlike love toward one another, the church's internal life becomes a powerful testimony. The surrounding community can see tangible evidence of the transforming power of the gospel through the relationships within the body of Christ.

Digital Presence as Cultural Expression

In the modern world, a church's digital presence has become an extension of its public witness. Websites, social media platforms, livestreams, and online communication now function as visible expressions of the congregation's identity and priorities. What the church communicates through these channels often shapes how the surrounding community understands its mission and character.

Matthew 5:16 (KJV) records the instruction of Jesus: "Let your light so shine before men, that they may see your good works, and glorify your Father which is in heaven." The verse emphasizes that the visible actions of believers should reflect the character of God. In today's environment, that visibility often includes digital communication.

Digital platforms communicate cultural signals in several ways. The tone of messages, the subjects emphasized in posts, the imagery used in promotional materials, and the interactions between members online all contribute to the impression others form about the church. These elements collectively reveal what the congregation values and how it presents itself to the world.

A church's digital presence can therefore reinforce its mission when it reflects the same convictions expressed in its teaching and leadership. Posts that encourage spiritual growth, highlight acts of service, and communicate biblical truth demonstrate that the church's online communication aligns with its deeper purpose.

However, when digital communication focuses primarily on entertainment, promotion, or public image, the church's message may become less clear. The surrounding community may struggle to determine whether the church primarily offers an event-driven experience or a community devoted to spiritual transformation.

Leaders should therefore view digital communication as an extension of the church's culture rather than as a separate activity.

The same values that guide preaching, discipleship, and fellowship should also guide what the church chooses to communicate online.

Members also contribute to this digital witness through their personal interactions on social media. The way believers represent the church in public conversations, online discussions, and shared content influences how others perceive the faith community.

When digital presence reflects humility, integrity, and commitment to biblical truth, it strengthens the church's witness in the wider world. Online communication becomes another avenue through which the light of the gospel can be seen.

By treating digital communication as a cultural expression rather than merely a promotional tool, churches ensure that their public presence remains aligned with their convictions. In doing so, the message of the gospel continues to shine clearly both within the congregation and across the broader digital landscape.

Community Perception

The reputation of a church within its surrounding community reflects more than public messaging or promotional efforts. Community perception develops over time through the observable actions of the congregation and its leaders. The way a church serves, interacts, and conducts itself beyond its walls influences how the broader public understands its mission and character.

1 Peter 2:12 (KJV) provides guidance for how believers should conduct themselves among those outside the faith: "Having your conversation honest among the Gentiles: that, whereas they speak against you as evildoers, they may by your good works, which they shall behold, glorify God in the day of visitation." The passage emphasizes that the conduct of believers should demonstrate integrity and goodness in the presence of those who do not share their faith.

Consistent patterns of behavior shape community perception. Acts of service, kindness toward neighbors, ethical business practices, and genuine concern for others' well-being all contribute to the church's reputation. These visible expressions of faith help communicate the character of the congregation to the surrounding community.

Conversely, when a church becomes known primarily for internal conflict, leadership controversy, or inconsistent conduct, its public witness can be weakened. Even if such issues occur in only a small portion of the congregation, they may still influence how those outside it view the church.

For this reason, leaders must consider the broader impact of the church's actions. Decisions made within the congregation often carry consequences that extend beyond the immediate community of believers. The church's reputation influences how its message is received by those observing from the outside.

Members also contribute to this public perception through their everyday lives. The conduct of believers in workplaces, neighborhoods, schools, and community activities reflects the values they have learned within the church. Their actions extend the church's cultural identity.

Healthy churches seek to maintain a reputation marked by integrity, service, and humility. While the church cannot control every opinion formed by others, it can ensure that its conduct consistently reflects the teachings of Scripture.

When the church's culture aligns with biblical conviction, the surrounding community begins to see evidence of faith expressed in action. In this way, the church's public reputation becomes part of its witness, demonstrating the practical influence of the gospel in its members' lives.

Distinction From the World

The church is called to live within the world while maintaining a distinct identity shaped by the truth of Scripture. Believers interact with society, work within its structures, and serve their communities, yet their values and conduct are intended to reflect a different set of convictions. This distinction forms an important part of the church's witness.

2 Corinthians 6:17 (KJV) expresses this calling clearly: "Wherefore come out from among them, and be ye separate, saith the Lord, and touch not the unclean thing; and I will receive you." The instruction emphasizes that the people of God are not to adopt the moral and spiritual patterns of the surrounding culture. Instead, they are called to live according to God's standards.

Distinction does not mean isolation from society. The church remains engaged in the world through service, compassion, and the proclamation of the gospel. Believers are called to love their neighbors and demonstrate the character of Christ within their communities. However, this engagement must occur without abandoning the convictions that define Christian life.

Cultural distinction becomes visible through patterns of behavior, speech, and decision-making. Members of the church demonstrate honesty, humility, and moral integrity even when such qualities may differ from the prevailing values of the broader culture. These choices reveal the influence of biblical teaching within the life of the congregation.

When this distinction is maintained, the church offers a clear example of a community shaped by faith. Observers can see that the church's beliefs are reflected in its members' everyday conduct. This consistency strengthens the credibility of the church's witness.

Conversely, when the church gradually adopts the values or practices of the surrounding culture without careful discernment, its identity can become less clear. Members and observers alike may struggle to recognize what distinguishes the church from the society around it.

For this reason, leaders must continually reinforce the convictions that define the church's identity. Teaching, discipleship, and governance should all encourage believers to live according to biblical standards while remaining engaged in compassionate service to others.

When the church preserves this balance, it fulfills its calling to be both present in the world and distinct from it. The congregation becomes a visible community shaped by the truth of Scripture, demonstrating through its conduct the transforming influence of the gospel.

Faithfulness Under Scrutiny

Faithfulness becomes most visible when the church is observed closely by others. Leadership decisions, congregational behavior, and the consistency of biblical teaching are all scrutinized both within the church and by the surrounding community. During such moments, the integrity of the church's culture is revealed.

1 Corinthians 4:2 (KJV) states, "Moreover it is required in stewards, that a man be found faithful." The apostle Paul reminds believers that those entrusted with responsibility must demonstrate reliability and integrity in fulfilling that trust. Stewardship in the church involves faithfully carrying out the responsibilities God gives, regardless of the circumstances.

In the life of the church, scrutiny may arise in many forms. Leadership decisions may be questioned, cultural expectations may be tested, and the church's convictions may be challenged by changing societal pressures. These moments reveal whether the church's commitments are firmly grounded or easily altered.

Faithfulness requires consistency between stated belief and observable action. Leaders must demonstrate that their decisions align with the convictions they proclaim. Congregational life must reflect the same biblical standards taught from the pulpit. When actions and teaching remain aligned, the church displays integrity even under critical scrutiny.

Scrutiny can also serve a refining purpose. When leaders respond with humility, clarity, and adherence to Scripture, the church’s witness may actually grow stronger. Observers often recognize when individuals remain faithful to their convictions despite pressure to compromise.

However, when leaders respond to scrutiny by abandoning principles or concealing the truth, cultural trust begins to erode. Members may become uncertain about the reliability of leadership, and the church’s testimony within the community may weaken.

For this reason, faithfulness must remain a central priority in church leadership and congregational life. The goal is not to avoid scrutiny, but to ensure that when examination occurs, the church demonstrates integrity in its beliefs and actions.

A culture rooted in biblical conviction equips the church to withstand such moments. When leaders and members consistently pursue faithfulness, the church remains steady even when its conduct is closely observed. In this way, faithfulness under scrutiny becomes a visible testimony of the church’s commitment to the truth of Scripture.

Chapter Twenty The Visible Testimony of Governance

The culture of a church is never accidental. It develops over time through the repeated decisions, teachings, and behaviors that leadership allows, encourages, and corrects. While many churches speak about culture as something abstract or emotional, culture is actually the visible evidence of how leadership governs the life of the congregation.

Throughout this work, culture has been examined not as a program or personality trait, but as the outcome of convictions that are consistently lived out. Values define what leadership truly believes. Vision provides direction for where those convictions lead. Mission defines the work through which that direction is pursued. Strategy organizes that work, and policy protects it through clear guardrails. Culture emerges as the shared behavioral environment that develops as these elements function together.

Because culture grows from these structural realities, it cannot be produced simply by enthusiasm or by the desire to appear welcoming or relevant. Culture forms as people repeatedly observe what leadership rewards, tolerates, and corrects. Over time, these repeated signals shape the congregation's expectations and habits.

When leadership convictions remain clear and consistently reinforced, culture becomes stable and recognizable. Members understand how the church operates and what behaviors are expected. The life of the congregation reflects the priorities that leadership has chosen to uphold.

When leadership convictions weaken or become inconsistent, culture gradually drifts. Confusion begins to appear in ministries, expectations become unclear, and the congregation's behavior no longer reflects the principles the church claims to hold. In such cases, cultural instability often reveals deeper issues within governance and leadership structure.

For this reason, culture should be understood as the visible testimony of governance. The church's everyday conduct demonstrates whether leadership is faithfully stewarding the responsibilities entrusted to it. Culture reveals whether convictions are being upheld or quietly neglected.

Healthy churches recognize that culture is not managed primarily through slogans or messaging. It is shaped through faithful leadership, biblical teaching, and consistent accountability. When governance remains aligned with Scripture and is reinforced through daily practice, the church's culture becomes a living reflection of those convictions.

The chapters of this work have explored the many signals through which culture is formed, preserved, or corrupted. Leadership behavior, worship environment, speech patterns, financial priorities, governance structure, and disciplinary practices all communicate powerful messages about what the church truly values.

Ultimately, the church's culture becomes a testimony. It testifies to what the congregation believes about God, holiness, authority, and its mission in the world. The question is not whether culture exists within the church, but whether that culture faithfully reflects the truths the church proclaims.

Conviction Made Visible

Convictions within the church must eventually become visible through action. Beliefs that remain only in written statements or verbal affirmations cannot shape the life of a congregation unless they are demonstrated through consistent behavior.

James 2:18 (KJV) declares, "Yea, a man may say, Thou hast faith, and I have works: shew me thy faith without thy works, and I will shew thee my faith by my works." The passage emphasizes that true faith becomes evident through the actions that accompany it. Faith is not merely professed but demonstrated.

This principle applies directly to the life of the church. Values and doctrinal convictions provide the foundation for church identity, but those convictions must be reflected through the choices leaders make and the behaviors the congregation practices.

When leadership consistently reinforces biblical priorities, those convictions gradually become embedded in the life of the church. Members observe how decisions are made, how conflicts are handled, and how ministries operate. Through these repeated experiences, the convictions of the church become visible.

Conversely, when stated convictions remain disconnected from leadership behavior, the congregation quickly recognizes the inconsistency. Over time, written statements lose their influence, and culture begins to form around what leaders actually practice rather than what they claim to believe.

For this reason, leaders must ensure that the convictions they teach are also the convictions they demonstrate. The credibility of church leadership depends upon this consistency. When conviction and conduct remain aligned, the church's culture reflects the faith it proclaims.

Authority Lived Out

Authority within the church is not merely positional. It is expressed through the faithful exercise of responsibility under the authority of Christ. Leaders are entrusted with influence and responsibility, and the manner in which they exercise that authority shapes the congregation's culture.

Colossians 3:17 (KJV) instructs believers, "And whatsoever ye do in word or deed, do all in the name of the Lord Jesus, giving thanks to God and the Father by him." This command reminds the church that every action should reflect submission to Christ and gratitude for His work.

When leaders understand their authority as a stewardship under Christ, their decisions reflect humility and responsibility. Authority becomes a tool for service rather than a matter of personal preference. Leaders guide the church with clarity while recognizing that they remain accountable to God.

The way authority is exercised influences the entire culture of the church. When authority is exercised responsibly, members experience clarity, order, and trust. When authority is neglected or misused, confusion and instability often follow.

Healthy churches cultivate leadership that understands authority as a responsibility to be lived out faithfully. Leaders model obedience to Christ, and the congregation learns through their example how to live under that same authority.

Stewardship Before God

Every leader within the church carries a responsibility that ultimately extends beyond human accountability. Leadership decisions affect the spiritual direction of the congregation and therefore carry serious weight before God.

Romans 14:12 (KJV) reminds believers of this reality: "So then every one of us shall give account of himself to God." The passage emphasizes that each person will one day stand before God to give an account for their actions.

For church leaders, this responsibility includes the stewardship of doctrine, governance, and congregational life. Leaders are entrusted with guiding the church in accordance with biblical principles, ensuring that the congregation remains faithful to its calling.

Recognizing this accountability encourages careful and prayerful leadership. Decisions are made not merely for immediate convenience but with an awareness of long-term spiritual consequences. Leaders consider how their choices will influence the church's witness and integrity.

Stewardship before God reminds leaders that their work is not simply organizational management. It is a spiritual responsibility that affects others' lives and reflects the church's faithfulness to Christ.

When leaders remain mindful of this accountability, they approach governance with humility, seriousness, and devotion to Scripture.

The Future of the Local Church

The long-term health of the church depends upon its commitment to remain faithful to the authority of Christ and the teachings of Scripture. While cultural trends and social pressures may change over time, the church's calling remains constant.

Ephesians 5:27 (KJV) describes Christ's purpose for His church: "That he might present it to himself a glorious church, not having spot, or wrinkle, or any such thing; but that it should be holy and without blemish." The ultimate future of the church is defined by its relationship with Christ.

Local congregations participate in this greater purpose by pursuing holiness, faithfulness, and obedience in their present context. The decisions leaders make today determine whether future generations inherit a church grounded in biblical truth.

Churches that maintain clear convictions, disciplined governance, and faithful teaching provide stability for the next generation of believers. Their culture encourages spiritual growth and prepares future leaders to continue the church's work.

Conversely, when cultural drift weakens conviction and governance becomes inconsistent, the long-term health of the church may suffer. Future generations may inherit confusion rather than clarity.

For this reason, leaders must consider the future implications of the culture they are shaping today. The structures, habits, and convictions reinforced within the church will influence its direction for years to come.

Final Charge to Leaders

The responsibility of church leadership ultimately centers on faithfulness to the Word of God. Leaders are entrusted with teaching, guiding, and correcting the congregation in accordance with the authority of Scripture.

2 Timothy 4:2 (KJV) provides this final charge: "Preach the word; be instant in season, out of season; reprove, rebuke, exhort with all longsuffering and doctrine." The instruction calls on leaders to remain steadfast in proclaiming the truth, regardless of circumstances.

Leadership within the church requires courage and compassion. There will be seasons when biblical teaching is welcomed and seasons when it is resisted. In both cases, leaders must remain faithful to their calling.

The work of shaping church culture cannot be separated from this responsibility. Teaching the Word, correcting errors, encouraging faithfulness, and guiding the congregation with patience all contribute to the development of a healthy church culture.

When leaders fulfill this responsibility faithfully, the church remains grounded in truth and strengthened in unity. The congregation learns to pursue obedience to Christ and to live in accordance with Scripture.

This charge serves as both encouragement and a reminder. The work of leadership carries great responsibility, but it also participates in the enduring mission of Christ's church.

Faithful leadership, guided by Scripture and sustained by conviction, allows the church to remain steady in its calling. Through such leadership, the church's culture continues to reflect the truth it proclaims.

www.ingramcontent.com/pod-product-compliance
Lightning Source LLC
La Vergne TN
LVHW090604110826
845146LV00001B/256

* 9 7 9 8 9 9 4 5 0 4 1 6 1 *